FORM AND STYLE IN

Thesis Writing

WILLIAM GILES CAMPBELL

FORMERLY OF THE UNIVERSITY OF SOUTHERN CALIFORNIA

HOUGHTON MIFFLIN COMPANY · BOSTON · NEW YORK

CHICAGO · DALLAS · ATLANTA · SAN FRANCISCO · The Riverside Press Cambridge

ACKNOWLEDGMENTS

For their help in preparing the earlier work on which the present one is based, the author wishes to express his appreciation to Drs. Clarence M. Case, Owen C. Coy, Frank H. Garver, Allison Gaw, H. W. Hill, Osman R. Hull, Albert S. Raubenheimer, and Frederick J. Weersing, all of The University of Southern California.

Most deeply and most directly, the author is indebted to his wife, Carolyn Swetland Campbell, whose numerous suggestions, wise counsel, and stimulus to scholarship have contributed so greatly to the present work.

PREFACE

IN ITS original form, this book was the outgrowth of a need experienced in a single department in a single university, a need for some simple codification of the stylistic and mechanical problems involved in putting a thesis into final shape. As its content was seen increasingly to apply beyond the bounds of that department and that university, it was broadened in scope and issued in 1939 as *A Form Book for Thesis Writing*, a manual devoted to answering the questions encountered by thesis writers and thesis typists in all fields and in all universities.

With the development of greater specialization in the form and techniques of thesis preparation in the various fields, new opportunities for usefulness in a book of this kind have opened up. Further, its widespread use in the preparation of undergraduate papers has suggested ways in which it might be still more helpfully oriented to papers at the course level. Thus out of years of experience with the former edition, and out of hundreds of suggestions made for its revision, has emerged this new edition, *Form and Style in Thesis Writing*, designed to extend and expand the usefulness of its predecessor.

The book has not been radically altered, but where changes and additions have been made, they stem directly from the needs and demands of those who have been using the book. For example, the relatively large number of theses being written in mathematics and the sciences has made it desirable to include more information on accepted standard and variant forms of reference in these fields, so that the student may be spared some of the labor of checking for usage among journals.

The current wide use of graphic illustrations, moreover, has suggested that fairly detailed information might well be given on the preparation of these materials, with some indication of how to determine the most appropriate graphic form for the writer's purpose, and how to relate tables and illustrations most effectively to context.

Another significant change from the earlier edition, in an effort to make the book easier to use, is the placement of facsimile examples of footnote and bibliographical forms with the instructions relating to them, in Chapter 4. Supplementing these, a check list of facsimile entries is given at the back of the book as well, for quick reference by topic and problem.

Finally, since many universities, junior colleges, and even high schools require that standard form be followed in the preparation of course and term papers, added emphasis has been placed on the points of minor difference between theses and undergraduate reports, in order to help these students adapt the requirements of thesis form and style to their needs.

WILLIAM GILES CAMPBELL

TABLE OF CONTENTS

Chapter **4**

FOOTNOTE AND BIBLIOGRAPHICAL REFERENCES

Chapter **5**

TABLES AND ILLUSTRATIONS

Chapter 6

TYPING AIDS

Chapter 7

MATTERS OF STYLE

BIBLIOGRAPHY

APPENDIX

1 | GENERAL CONSIDERATIONS

A THESIS IS A STANDARD REQUIREMENT of American colleges and universities for nearly every postgraduate degree and an ever-increasing number of undergraduate degrees. Throughout this book, it will be assumed that the reader is undertaking the preparation of a thesis, a term paper, or some other formal report of an investigation he has conducted.

At as early a date as possible, the student should consult the departmental adviser or other official designated to counsel with him about the entire program for the academic year, including the thesis requirement. This will allow satisfactory planning of time for both research and course work. Close attention should also be paid to the bulletin of the institution, for it usually contains information on the number of copies of the thesis to be prepared, the local requirements for forms of acceptance, and the date when final copies must be turned in for a degree to be granted at the ensuing convocation.

I. THE THESIS PROGRAM

Research procedures

● No attempt will here be made to indicate the manner of selecting a problem or of outlining a project for research work; that task is left to the chairman of the thesis committee, or to the whole committee. The student may find it profitable, however, to read some standard work on research techniques either before consulting his thesis committee or while his study is in progress. A list of such aids will be found in the Bibliography, pages 68 to 70. The librarian or one of the professors in his major field may be able to suggest other guides suitably related to the investigation.

Writing aids

● It is generally assumed that a college senior or graduate has had sufficient practice in writing to guarantee his ability to use the English language with facility; therefore, with the exception of a few instances in which particular forms have been adopted for research or thesis writing, no attempt will be made to present materials dealing with the matter of *writing* the English language. It is suggested, however, that the student secure the following books and use them diligently in connection with the preparation of his thesis: (1) A handbook of composition, for example, *The Century Handbook of Writing*, Manly and Rickert's *The Writer's Index of Good Form and Good English*, Perrin's *Writer's Guide and Index to English*, Foerster and Steadman's *Writing and Thinking*, or Woolley's *College Handbook of Composition;* (2) a college dictionary, for example, Clarence L. Barnhart's *American College Dictionary* or the Merriam-Webster *Collegiate Dictionary;* (3) a thesaurus, for example, Roget's; and (4) a manual of style, for example, *A Manual of Style*, published by the University of Chicago Press. Additional books and manuals to help in the actual organization and writing of the manuscript are listed in the Bibliography, pages 68 to 70. No pains should be spared to make the thesis a scholarly contribution in every way, including language usage and accuracy of expression.

Criticism and suggestions

● An important part of the education that a student receives while writing a thesis consists of the criticisms and suggestions offered by the chairman of his committee. A student should expect and welcome constructive criticism from the one who is directing the writing of his thesis. Such criticism is given for the purpose of helping him improve the quality of his final product and should be accepted in the same spirit. Far from resenting criticism as reflecting upon his ability, the student should consider it part of the instruction for which he has paid and to which he is entitled. The university assumes that one who is fulfilling a thesis requirement is not capable of independent work at this point in his graduate career, and for this reason supplies guidance through the thesis committee. Were the student known to be an experienced and capable investigator, it is probable that he would not be required to write a thesis before being awarded an advanced degree.

II. THESIS FORM

It is the particular intent of this manual to present those matters of style and form not usually found in books devoted to techniques of research and of writing.

Standard thesis form

● There is not at the present time absolute agreement among authorities regarding details of form in thesis writing. Some of the reasons for these differences of opinion are entirely logical, so that, in a given situation, any one of several different usages might conceivably be satisfactory. In the preparation of this manual, when such disagreements have been noted, the practices proposed in *A Manual of Style*, of the University of Chicago Press, have generally been followed.

Some of the departments within a university have special forms that apply to work in only these departments or schools. In such cases, the chairman of the thesis committee should inform the student of deviations from the style here presented. For example, in the department of history, reference to documents or documentary evidence may require a unique arrangement; if so, the student should enlist the aid of his professor in preparing his thesis properly. The Bibliography in this manual (pages 68 to 70) supplies references that will be helpful to advanced students or to those working on problems that call for special forms.

Whether or not all the material here presented is used, the student should adopt that portion which may be employed without variation, add to it those forms that are prescribed by his adviser, and then follow the whole without deviation. Authorities may not agree on the exact form to be followed, but no authority sanctions the practice of using several different forms within the same manuscript.

Clarity has been the desideratum in the preparation of this guide. For special problems of form and style not covered by this or any other manual, the thesis writer will wish to be guided by this same consideration. Meaning should never be obscured by the use of confusing or unusual forms in handling quotations, footnotes, or other materials.

Manuals of style

● Out of necessity and through experience with written work, many of the larger institutions and organizations concerned with publication have developed rules of usage that meet the demands for clarity; several have published manuals of style in which these rules are set forth explicitly. Examples of these are *A Manual of Style*, published by the University of Chicago Press, and the *Style Manual* of the United States Government Printing Office; others will be found listed in the catalogue of any university library.

Many scholarly journals and associations, too, have prepared style sheets that cover problems peculiar to their fields; for example, the *Style Sheet* of the Modern Language Association of America and the *Author's Manual* of the *Duke Mathematical Journal*.

Explicit instructions

● The six ensuing chapters of this manual contain detailed instructions on thesis form and style. The assumption is that the writer of a thesis will be aided more by explicit instructions than by general suggestions.

Since the mass of details may seem forbidding to the reader and since the material is scattered throughout the many pages of this manual, a few words of reassurance are in order. The student may be certain that every form recommended has justified itself in practice and in the long run may be counted upon to save his time and patience. He will discover, moreover, that methods which look complicated when written in the form of directions are really simple when used.

Furthermore, the minuteness with which the rules for thesis work have been set down will make it easy for the student to acquire the habit of always employing the correct form. As a matter of fact, many of the usages recommended are doubtless already being followed by the typical graduate student. The habit of using the correct form may easily be developed if the student will study the directions given in this manual. Especially during the composition and revision of his thesis, he should look upon the information presented as a source for reference.

Sample pages

● Although a great deal of material has been included that will give, in expository form, the style to be followed, the student will also find it helpful to turn to the sample pages in the Appendix and follow these examples in his writing. Typists and others who prepare manuscripts for submission to the various departments within the university should follow in all their work the form used in the sample pages. In the majority of cases, a thesis will be required to conform to the standards set up in the samples. It must not be assumed, however, that mere excellence of form will guarantee the acceptance of a thesis or a dissertation.

III. TERM PAPERS

The correct method of presenting written work should be used by the student whether he is writing a thesis, a seminar report, or a term paper. Practice in the employment of correct form during his undergraduate years will lead to the formation of habits of correct usage that will prove of value during his graduate career.

There are some basic differences between term papers and theses, but these relate more to the nature of the problems involved and the research procedures followed than to the form of reporting the results obtained. A term paper is usually more limited in scope than a thesis; as a rule, the investigation is made in the library and seldom involves laboratory research or field study. Hence the organization of the term paper may be simplified because of its brevity; for example, many of the introductory elements of a thesis are entirely omitted in the usual term report. Whereas the hoped-for outcome of a graduate thesis is to push back the frontiers of knowledge, the undergraduate term paper seldom pretends to this seriousness of purpose and may have as its major aim giving the inexperienced student instruction and practice in research techniques and the methods of reporting results obtained. It often happens that a formal bibliography is not required in a term paper, if its footnotes contain full bibliographical data. The form of the two types of reports is basically the same; what may look like different styles consist of minor adjustments to the realities of brevity, limited scope, and the specific purposes of the term paper as compared with the more comprehensive thesis.

When a term paper is a course requirement, the instructor should stipulate the nature and extent of the work to be done and should indicate the ways, if any, in which the form will vary from that here outlined.

The idea that a term paper is stilted because thesis form is followed in its preparation is as erroneous as the belief that the use of good grammar in a personal letter indicates an unfriendly attitude on the part of the writer.

2 | FORMAT OF THE THESIS

THE MECHANICAL FORMAT of the thesis includes three categories of materials: the preliminaries, the text of the thesis, and the reference materials. The various components occur in the following order, although not every thesis includes all the items listed:

I. *The preliminaries*
Title-page
Approval sheet
Preface and/or acknowledgments (if desired)
Table of Contents
List of Tables (if any)
List of Figures or Illustrations (if any)

II. *The text of the thesis*
Introductory chapter, or chapters
Report of the study, appropriately divided into chapters and sections
Summary chapter, or chapters

III. *The reference materials*
Bibliography (in some theses the appendix precedes the bibliography)
Appendix, or appendixes (if any)
Index (if any)

Pagination of thesis

● Every page in a thesis is assigned a number, although not every page has its page number typed on it. There are two separate series of page numbers. The first, in small Roman numerals, begins with the title-page and ends with the last page preceding Chapter I; the second series, in Arabic numerals, begins with the first page of Chapter I and continues throughout the thesis, the bibliography, and the appendix or appendixes.

The initial page of any major subdivision of the thesis — such as the title-page, the first page of the table of contents, and the first page of a chapter — will have no page numeral placed on it, but a number will be allowed in the series for that page. For example, if the last page of Chapter I is nineteen, the first page of Chapter II is twenty, but the page numeral does not appear on it; the second page of Chapter II is twenty-one and is so numbered.

The page numbers, whether Arabic or small Roman, are conventionally placed four double spaces from the top of the paper, aligned with the right-hand margin.

I. THE PRELIMINARIES

Title-page

● The first page of a thesis or a dissertation is the title-page. Although the bookbinder may insert a blank sheet of paper between this page and the cover, the first typed page is counted as the first page of the manuscript.

The form of the title-page is usually prescribed by the bulletin of the graduate division of the university. It includes the title of the thesis, the designation of the faculty and the institution to which the thesis is submitted, the degree for which the thesis is presented, the full name of the candidate, and the month and year in which the degree is to be granted. This material is equivalent to the imprint of a book.

The title should be brief but accurate and comprehensive. It should be so phrased as accurately to limit the subject under discussion and promise no more than the investigation attempts to fulfill. A good rule is to try to include in the title all words or phrases under which, in an index, a scholar would search for a paper containing the particular material included in the report. Effective titles are usually composed of three or four main words or groups of words. As far as possible, the meaning should be clear at a glance. Also, to avoid awkward combinations of words, the euphony of the title should be considered.

Such titles as *An Inquiry into . . .* and *An Investigation of . . .* are modest and satisfactory. Titles that indicate the method of research employed are also desirable, as *A Historical Study of . . .*, *An Experimental Investigation of . . .*, and *A Survey of . . . .*

The following is a list of typical thesis titles:

An Investigation of the Financial Activities of the American Federation of Labor

A Survey of the Military Secondary Schools in the United States

An Analysis of the Influence of Ralph Waldo Emerson on Walt Whitman

A Critical History of the Principal English and American Theories Concerning the Social Utility of Bank Credit

A Discriminative Study of Methods for the Quantitative Determination of Fluorine

A Historical Study of Christianity as a Potent Factor in the Development of the Chinese Republic

An Experimental Study of the Effect of Length of Paragraph on Speed in Reading

The statement of submission, indicating to whom and for what degree the thesis is offered, follows the title. This information is centered, and is set half way down the page. The name of the writer and the month and year in which the degree is to be granted usually appear at the bottom of the title-page.

The exact location of this material and the spacing to be used may be seen on the sample title-pages in the Appendix, pages 75 to 77.

Approval sheet

● The form for the certificate of approval of the department faculty, the graduate council, or other appropriate authority follows the title-page. Customarily it is a thesis-size sheet of paper ($8\frac{1}{2} \times 11$ inches). The majority of institutions have a form printed for this purpose, and the matter is cared for by a departmental secretary. Sometimes the provision for signatures of approval is made on the title-page. The requirements of the institution should, in all cases, be ascertained and followed.

Preface and acknowledgments

● Preface, acknowledgments, and foreword are commonly treated as synonymous terms in the instance of a thesis. Such a preliminary section may contain a brief statement of the scope, aim, and general character of the research upon which the report is being made; it may consist solely of acknowledgments; or, especially at the level of course reports and the Master's degree, it may be omitted.

Acknowledgments recognize the persons to whom the writer is indebted for guidance and assistance and those to whom he is grateful for any special or nonroutine aid. The help rendered by the chairman and members of the student's committee is part of their regular work and does not require written appreciation, although in most cases the help given far exceeds any teaching-load requirement and should, as a matter of courtesy, be recognized. Good taste calls for acknowledgments to be expressed simply and tactfully.

Table of contents

● The analytical table of contents is the next separate section following the prefatory acknowledgment section, or the approval sheet if no section of acknowledgments is included. The table of contents lists the chapter (or section) headings into which the thesis is divided, and the main headings and subdivisions in each, with page citations. It provides the reader with an analytical overview of the material covered by the study, together with the order of presentation.

The relationship between main divisions and subdivisions is shown by the appropriate use of indention and capitalization. All headings (that is, entries) in the table of contents should correspond exactly in wording with the headings as they appear in the text. However, the Roman numeral of a centered head (see page 9) is not carried into the table of contents.

The main headings of the table of contents, which in theses and dissertations are the chapter titles, are written in full capitals, with no terminal punctuation, and are consecutively numbered in Roman caps. If a heading requires more than one line, the second and following lines are indented two spaces in from the first letter of the initial line and are double-spaced.

The subheadings of the main headings, which in theses and dissertations are the major divisions of individual chapters, are indented two spaces in from the initial letter of the first line of the main heading. When a subheading requires more than one line, the additional lines are underhung (indented) two spaces from the initial letter of the first line of the subheading. The initial letters of the first word and of all nouns, pronouns, adjectives, adverbs, and verbs are capitalized.

Subdivisions, if any, of the subheadings are indented two spaces from the initial letter of the first line of the preceding subheading. Second, or following, lines are underhung two spaces from the initial letter of the first line of its heading. Both in the body of the thesis and in the table of contents, only the first letters of the first word and of proper nouns are in caps.

All lines, including underhanging lines, are double-spaced. Leaders guide the eye to the page numbers which are aligned at the right.

The following illustration covers these points:

No terminal punctuation is used for the centered heading, TABLE OF CONTENTS (or, simply, CONTENTS), or for any other line of the table of contents.

The titles BIBLIOGRAPHY, APPENDIX(ES), and INDEX, if any, are included as main divisions of the table of contents. They follow the chapters, begin flush with the left-hand margin, and appear in full capital letters. The page number on which each of these begins is shown in the column at the right.

The capitalized words "CHAPTER" and "PAGE" head their respective columns, flush with the margins.

Examples of these rules may be seen in the samples, pages 78 and 79.

The table of contents should not be so detailed as to confuse the reader. In a thesis of average length not more than one or two pages need be devoted to it. There are times, however, when an exceedingly detailed table of contents is appropriate, and the number of items to be included is large. In such cases, the following condensed form may be used, with the permission of the chairman of the thesis committee:

List of tables

● After the table of contents, the next separate section, typed on a page, or pages, by itself, is the list of tables. This is made up of the captions of any comparative tables of figures included by the author to report his researches or to substantiate various points of his investigation.

For each table, the number of the table, its exact caption or title, and the number of the manuscript page on which it appears are given. The initial letters of important words in the captions are capitalized.

The tables are numbered consecutively with capital Roman numerals.

No terminal punctuation is used for the heading, LIST OF TABLES, or after any title listed therein.

The words "TABLE" and "PAGE," in full caps, head their respective columns, flush with the margins.

Examples of the application of these rules may be seen in the sample on page 80.

List of Figures or illustrations

● If any illustrations or graphs are used, the list of these constitutes the next consecutive separate section, and in it the practices listed above are followed, except that Figures are numbered with Arabic, rather than Roman, numbers.

If there are several illustrations of any one kind — for example, maps — it is proper to have a distinct series for them, numbered separately, and separately listed at this point in the thesis. A good rule to follow is to have a separate category for any type of illustration of which there are ten or more. Thus, if there were twelve maps, seven charts, two photographs, and three diagrams, there would be a list of maps, and all the other illustrations would be grouped together in a list of Figures.

The capitalized words "FIGURE," or "ILLUSTRATION," or "PLATE," and "PAGE" head their respective columns, flush with the margins.

A sample list of Figures may be seen on page 81.

II. THE TEXT OF THE THESIS

The thesis proper begins with the first page of Chapter I and follows the preliminaries detailed above. In most theses, the chapters may readily be divided into three categories: the introductory chapter, or chapters; the major report of the study, divided into logical chapter divisions; and the summary chapter, or chapters, which should contain the findings, conclusions, and recommendations of the report. The organization and distribution of content should be such that each chapter represents an important division of the subject investigated and reported.

**Introductory chapter
or chapters**

● The first chapter, or chapters, should contain the following:

1. A clear and complete statement of the problem investigated or the purpose of the study.

2. A validation or justification of the problem, which, by a discussion of discriminatingly selected reasons, establishes the importance of the problem. It is often appropriate, at this point, to indicate the limitations of the undertaking and to define words unique to the study or used in a restricted or unusual manner in reporting the investigation.

3. A preview of the organization of the remainder of the thesis. This will make it easy for the reader to see at a glance the relationship between the various parts of the work.

4. A résumé of the history and present status of the problem by means of a brief critical review of previous investigations of this and closely related problems. The contribution of each of these to the question as a whole should be made clear, together with the fact that the investigation now in progress arises from the fallacies or inadequacies of earlier studies.

5. A statement of the sources of data, the method of procedure (experimental technique), and the treatment of the findings. In a thesis of an experimental nature, a separate chapter is ordinarily devoted to these topics.

Report of the study

● It is impossible to give specific directions for organizing the findings of all studies, because of the wide variety of topics investigated, techniques employed, and kinds of data accumulated. Suffice to say that the chapters of this portion of the thesis *are the thesis* — they are the student's contribution to knowledge. All other portions of the manuscript are subordinate to what actually has been discovered and is here being made known. The student should, therefore, take great pains to present his material in a clear and orderly fashion, in terms that will be readily understood.

Final chapter

● The final chapter, or chapters, should be a summary, restating the developments of previous chapters and showing succinctly the more important findings and conclusions of the whole study. The author may list unanswered questions that have occurred to him but which require research beyond the limits of the undertaking reported.

General considerations

● Each chapter, other than the introductory and final chapters, should open with a paragraph or two containing (*a*) a statement of the portion of the problem to which the chapter is devoted, (*b*) a description of the materials and methods used in connection with this part of the investigation, and (*c*) an enumeration of the points to be covered.

In many theses, the concluding section of each chapter will consist of a summary indicating the contribution of that chapter to the whole study.

Each chapter must begin on a new page.

On the fifth double space below the top edge of the paper and centered on the typed matter, the chapter number, in full capitals with Roman numerals — for example, CHAPTER III — is placed.[1]

Three single spaces below the chapter-number heading, the chapter title is placed, also centered and in full caps. If the title requires more than one line, additional lines are double-spaced. The chapter title should show clearly what material is contained in the chapter and should reflect the fact that the chapter is a definite and logical division of the report.

---

[1] Here and elsewhere in this manual where rules for the physical appearance and set-up of the typescript page are given, it should be understood that these do not apply to the printed book. Book format and typescript format do have some elements in common; but book design, drawing as it does on the resources of typography and printing, is an art in itself, working in a different medium and solving problems of format and display in different ways.

The first line of the text begins three single spaces below the chapter title. Chapters may be subdivided into sections. If only one level of subdivision is necessary, either the centered head or the paragraph sidehead may be used; if two levels, both the centered head and the paragraph sidehead may be used. If a more elaborate system of subdivision is required, three levels are provided by use of the centered head (first level), free-standing sidehead (second level), and paragraph sidehead (third level), as follows:

I.   CENTERED HEAD

The centered head introduces a major division of the chapter. It is numbered with a Roman numeral and written in full capitals.

Free-standing Sidehead

The free-standing sidehead, set flush to the left margin and on a line by itself, introduces a subdivision of that part of the discussion begun under the centered head.

Paragraph sidehead. The paragraph sidehead provides for still another subdivision of the discussion, subordinate to both the centered head and the free-standing sidehead.

The student should be careful, however, to use subheadings only when they contribute in a functional way to his presentation. They should never be used as means of piecing out inadequacies in the organization and exposition of the thesis. All subheadings, in fact, should be removable without damage to the completeness of the text. Complete integrity of the text should be secured by providing for adequate transitions; these may be sections, paragraphs, or sentences, as the particular situation requires. Introductory and summary statements and complete topic sentences for each paragraph are often necessary to insure completeness of presentation.

Sample opening pages of chapters may be seen on pages 83 and 86 of the Appendix.

III. THE REFERENCE MATERIALS

The reference materials for every thesis include a bibliography and may embody an appendix, or appendixes, and an index.

Bibliography   ● The bibliography follows the body of the text and is a separate section of the thesis. It is preceded by a division sheet containing the single capitalized word BIBLIOG‑RAPHY, and is paged continuously with the text in Arabic numerals, since the reference matter is as much an integral part of the format as is any other section. In arranging the various elements on the contents page, care must be taken to prevent the bibliography from appearing to be subordinate to the last chapter, rather than a reference device for the whole thesis. The title, BIBLIOGRAPHY, is listed in the table of contents in full capitals, flush with the left-hand margin.

There are problems that have little literature; for them, few titles are listed in the bibliography. Some institutions require the writer to place the bibliography *before* the text of the manuscript, or to place appropriate references at the ends of the chapters to which they most pertinently apply. Recommended thesis practice, however, is for the bibliography to come at the end of the body of the text, preceded by a division sheet as indicated above.

Sample pages of bibliographies will be found in the Appendix, pages 102 and 103.

Appendix

● If an appendix is needed, it follows the bibliography and is preceded by a division sheet marked APPENDIX.

Original data, tables that present data of minor importance (as distinguished from those presenting major data which are included in the text), very lengthy quotations, supportive legal decisions or laws, and pertinent documents that are not readily available to the reader are placed in the appendix. Supplementary illustrative materials, such as forms and documents, may also be included. By shifting tables and other matter to the appendix, the body of the thesis may be kept from becoming unduly bulky.

Frequently an appendix offers a check upon the validity of the data of the thesis, and may also include materials that cannot readily be reproduced in the text. The appendix may be subdivided according to the classification of the materials included, especially if they are heterogeneous. Each such section should be listed by letter and title in the table of contents, for example:

APPENDIX A.   Clinical Charts   169

APPENDIX B.   Complete Case Histories for Subjects. . .   186

Index

● If an index is included, it follows the appendix or appendixes. An index is not required in an unpublished thesis; but if the thesis can be made more useful to the reader by an index, it may well have one. If the work is to be published as a book, a bulletin, or a monograph, an index is advisable; in the case of a work of any considerable complexity, it is indispensable.

Abstract of thesis

● Most universities require the doctoral candidate to prepare and submit also a separate abstract or digest of his thesis. An abstract consists of (1) a short statement of the problem; (2) a brief exposition of the methods and procedures employed in gathering the data; and (3) a condensed summary of the findings of the study. Usually there is no need to include a bibliography. Since local regulations vary on such matters as the length of the abstract and the number of copies required, information on these points should be obtained from the thesis committee or departmental secretary.

The title page may be the same as for the thesis proper, except that the expression, "An Abstract of a Thesis," is substituted for "A Thesis."

IV. FORMAT OF A TERM PAPER OR SEMINAR REPORT

A term paper or a seminar report may well be thought of as a "baby thesis." By following the general plan of the sample title-pages shown on pages 75 to 77, but substituting the words "A report submitted in partial fulfillment of the course requirements of Psychology 209" (or whatever the course may be) for the statement of submission normally used with theses and dissertations, a title-page of utility and neat appearance will be achieved.

Only infrequently do these less-formal reports require a preface, acknowledgments, an appendix, or an index.

If the structure of the report is complex enough to warrant subdivisions, a table of contents will be of help to the reader and will allow the instructor quickly and easily to comprehend the organization of what he is about to read. Appropriate subdivisions (often called parts or sections, rather than chapters) should be clearly indicated and handled in the same general style as for a thesis.

The same rules for spacing, indention, capitalization, and underscoring hold for term papers, seminar reports, theses, dissertations, and reports of all kinds. Common practice is for the professor to brief each class on the exact style expected, using this manual as a basic guide.

3

QUOTATIONS

In THESIS WRITING, quotations are used to convey information, to substantiate a point by using the words of an accepted authority, or to amplify a discussion by presenting the thinking of those who hold the same or differing views regarding the point being made.

If a thesis or a term paper is to avoid giving the impression of being a mere compilation of the words of other writers, quotations should be used sparingly; for in addition to being an accurate presentation of data, a research study must represent an original critical analysis or the contribution of a fresh method of interpreting and handling materials. Certain types of reports, however, such as an analysis of the works of some author, require more quotations than others.

Upon decision to make use of a given passage, the thesis writer must determine whether the excerpt should be paraphrased or quoted directly. A careful paraphrase that does complete justice to the source is usually preferable to a long quotation.

No thesis can be considered complete unless its author unmistakably and fully recognizes his indebtedness for every quotation used. If a footnote is employed for this purpose, its superscript, or raised numeral, follows the final punctuation of the matter. Examples of this practice may be seen on pages 86 to 88.

Length of quotations
● An excerpt from a periodical, a book, or a report should be as short as possible, rarely occupying more than one-half of a thesis page, and almost never more than one full page. Since long quotations are single-spaced, they show up better in the text if they do not fill a page. When a quotation covers more than a full page, the reader may easily forget whether he is reading an excerpt or the writer's own material. Further, a very long quotation is likely to contain some matter that is not strictly relevant and thus may actually obscure rather than illuminate the point at hand. The guiding consideration in fixing the length of the borrowed material should be a determination of the minimum amount that can be quoted without spoiling the original context and still achieve the purpose for which it is used. When very long quotations seem out of place in the body of the thesis yet essential to the whole presentation, they may be placed in the appendix and referred to at the proper points in the text.

Direct quotations
● Direct quotation should be employed (1) when giving the wording of laws, official rulings, and important edicts; (2) when citing mathematical, scientific, and other formulas; (3) when the exact words of a writer are absolutely essential; and (4) when a significant thought has been expressed with unusual felicity.

Any matter that is directly quoted must be reproduced exactly in all details — spelling, capitalization, punctuation, and paragraphing. This general rule holds good for quotations from dramas as well as from other works, although for dramatic excerpts the absence from the typewriter of small capitals will necessitate the substitution of underlined lower case, as for italics, where small capitals are used for speech headings and the like. If the material finally goes from the typewritten copy to print, however, the original form of the source must be restored. Careful comparison with first sources should always be made to check the accuracy of direct quotations. In the case of well-known authors, care should be taken to use the accepted standard edition of the work in question, or if that is not available, to specify the edition that has been used. Any corrections or remarks inserted by the person quoting should be carefully indicated. (See Interpolation, page 16.)

Short direct quotations

● Direct quotations not over three typewritten lines in length are enclosed in quotation marks and are run into the text. The sample pages in the Appendix of this manual and the portion of Chapter 7 that deals with punctuation should be referred to for illustrations of the proper method of inserting quotations and punctuating them.

An exception is made in the case of short quotations that, for the sake of emphasis, should stand out from the rest of the context. These, like long quotations, may be blocked-in, single-spaced, and indented.

Long direct quotations

● If a quotation is more than three typewritten lines in length, it is set off from the text in a separate paragraph, or paragraphs, indented four spaces, and single-spaced. (This method of placing the material on the page also indicates that it is to be set in smaller type if printed.) Opening and closing quotation marks are omitted in this single-spaced form, since this may be done without sacrificing clarity.

The paragraphing of the original text should be followed in quotations. A double space is provided between paragraphs of quoted material, even though the lines within each paragraph are single-spaced.

The conventional sequence of double and single quotation marks is used for quotes *within* the direct quotation, and also the usual forms of ellipsis and interpolation, whether the single-spaced or the double-spaced form is followed. That is, the first quote within a double-spaced quotation (which opens with double quotation marks) is introduced by a single quotation mark; and the first quote within a single-spaced quotation (which is not set off with quotation marks) is introduced by a double quotation mark.

Poetry quotations

● Unless unusual emphasis is desired, a part of a line, or a line, of poetry should be enclosed in quotation marks and run into the text. Two lines may be run into the text in the same way, if the lines are separated by a virgule (/):

Tennyson aptly expressed the idea when he said, "By

faith and faith alone embrace/Believing where we cannot

prove."

Verse quotations not run on should be introduced by a colon, centered on the page (the longest of the quoted lines is used to determine centering), and single-spaced. Quotation marks are omitted, unless they appear in the original:

In one of Tennyson's best-known works, "In Memoriam,"

an illustration of this point may be seen:

    But open converse is there none,
    So much the vital spirits sink
    To see the vacant chair, and think,
    "How good! how kind! and he is gone."

Quotations in footnotes

● When a short quotation occurs in a footnote, it is single-spaced, set in quotation marks, and punctuated exactly as in the original.

Although it is generally recommended that long prose quotations not included in the text itself be shifted to the appendix, there are some occasions when the thesis writer will want to place them in footnotes. The normal procedure is to single-space such quotations, double-space between paragraphs, enclose the quotation in quotation marks (place them before the start of the first line of each paragraph and at the end of the last line of the last paragraph), but indent only the first line of each paragraph (regular paragraph indention).

Poetry quoted in a footnote should be treated exactly as in the text proper.

Capitalization and punctuation of quotations

● Although the rule is that quoted materials be reproduced exactly, not only for context but also for capitalization, punctuation, and spelling, good grammatical practice will lead to two exceptions:

1. The first word of a quotation should not be capitalized, although it is in the original, if it forms a grammatical whole with what precedes it:

```
He would have agreed with Bacon that "a mixture of a lie

doth ever add pleasure."
```

If, however, the quotation follows a complete statement, the first letter is capitalized as in the original:

```
Bacon exhibits a similar strain of Machiavellian realism

when he says, "A mixture of a lie doth ever add pleasure."
```

2. The rules for punctuation marks as they relate to quotation marks (page 67, rule 8) are followed, irrespective of how the terminal punctuation appears in the original.

Quoting oral discourse

● Statements taken from a lecture or a personal interview should be submitted for the approval of the person who made them before they are incorporated into a thesis. This practice minimizes inaccuracies in quoting, and it insures the one using them against any breach of confidence on his part.

Credit for such a quotation is often given directly in the text, for example:

```
Dr. Howard Smith, in the commencement address deliv-

ered at Bixby College, June, 1946, said, "The young people

of today will find the world more exhausted than ever before

in modern history."
```

When the credit is not easily run into the text, or when such a complete reference detracts from the ease and smoothness of reading, a footnote containing adequate information should be used. If permission to quote has been secured, mention may well be made of this fact, for example:

Many leaders are prone to express excessive pessimism in public utterances, as is illustrated by the following statement: "The young people of today will find the world more exhausted than ever before in modern history."[1]

---

[1]President Howard Smith, of Bixby College, in a commencement address, June, 1946. Permission to quote secured.

Indirect quotations (paraphrases)

● When another person's ideas but not his exact words are used, full credit must be given as in the case of direct quotations.   Indirect quotations should not be enclosed in quotation marks. The footnote superscript is placed at the end of the paraphrased matter, whether or not the name of the author appears in the context. The cautions given above with regard to the validation of every quotation also apply here, for example:

Both Emory and Russell advance the theory that even in the realm of physics there are no absolutes, that the curve of mathematical probability may with accuracy be applied to these reactions.[2]

---

[2]William C. Emory, History of Mathematics (Atlanta: The Eastern Press, 1946), p. 261; and Thomas Russell, The Philosophy of Science (London: Evan Roberts and Sons, 1949), pp. 126-29.

Here the footnote properly contains two citations: one to Emory and one to Russell, exactly as though their word-for-word statements had been used in the thesis.

Ellipses

● Omissions in quoted matter are permitted if the original meaning is not altered. These should be indicated by the customary sign of ellipsis, alternating spaces and periods (. . .). Three dots alternating with spaces are used to indicate omission of material up to one paragraph in length. If the omitted material follows the end of a sentence, the three dots are *in addition* to the period that ends the preceding sentence. Omission of a full paragraph, or more than one paragraph, is shown by a full line of alternating periods and spaces extending across the page. The use of hyphens or asterisks instead of the periods in this connection is *never* permissible.

When quotation marks are used at the beginning or at the end of ellipses, the periods are enclosed within the marks, because they are considered part of the quotation.

Illustrations of the use of ellipses at the beginning, in the middle, and at the end of sentences, and of their use when at least a full paragraph is omitted, may be seen in the following selection:

```
    . . . Cell division can thus increase the length of
the filament . . . by adding to the total number of
cells, but this is merely growth of the individual and
is not production of a new organism.

. . . . . . . . . . . . . . . . . . . . . . . .

    After swimming around aimlessly for some time, the
spores come to rest at the bottom of the stream.  There
they behave as any cell might behave. . . .
```

Excessive use of ellipses at the beginning and end of quotations may be avoided by using the phrase, "in part," within the statement that introduces the quoted material.

Interpolation

● Since exact reproduction of all direct quotations is necessary, any corrections or original remarks by the person quoting should be inserted in square brackets [ ] at the proper point. Where the typewriter does not contain brackets, the device of employing parentheses instead should *never* be resorted to, but brackets should be neatly inserted with a pen and India ink.

Corrections within quoted matter can be made (1) by interpolating *sic* (Latin for "thus" — used to indicate accuracy of quoting when an error in fact is evident) in square brackets at the point of error; (2) by merely inserting the correction in square brackets immediately after the error; or (3) by adding in square brackets a phrase indicating the correction. The three methods occur in the following illustration:

```
    The Spanish legions rose in insurrection, and under
the leadership of the Emperor Galba, a cripple, they
advanced upon Rome in A.D. 86 [sic]; or, . . . in
A.D. 86 [68]; or, . . . in A.D. 86 [the correct date
is 68].
```

The italicizing of any part of a quotation not italicized in the original must also be indicated by the insertion of a phrase within square brackets or by the insertion of a footnote showing that the italics are those of the one quoting and not of the original author. Italics that occur in the original may similarly be indicated, in order to reassure the reader. Both types of italics appear in the following example:

```
    Five centuries have not weakened the pulse of life in
one of the Canterbury pilgrims, and the grave Knight and
the gay Squire, the genteel Prioress and the vulgar Wife
of Bath are living as when their palfreys raised the
dust on Kentish roads [italics not in the original].
There are some classes of Scott's characters, however,
whose original anemia [italics in the original] has
proved fatal to them.
```

Introductory phrases

● In order to avoid the constant use of some stereotyped phrase, such as "he says," an effort should be made to vary the manner of introducing short double-spaced direct quotations. A common method of varying the formal introduction is to quote directly up to the first natural pause and then to insert an introductory statement to identify the speaker. This pause may come at the end of the first phrase of the sentence, or even after the first word. Still another device is to invert the order of the phrase, as, for example, "says Pollard." In some types of written work, it is occasionally possible to add informative or descriptive matter, at the point of identification, to increase interest, as in the following quotation:

"It is intensely interesting," wrote Darwin, at the age of twenty-two, "how readily organisms may be divided into logical categories on the basis of structural elements."

The introductory phrase for a long single-spaced direct quotation is treated as part of the paragraph that precedes the selection. Although the difficulty of varying phrases of this type may be somewhat greater than with short double-spaced direct quotations, the monotonous use of a single form should be avoided. A colon usually follows such a phrase, thus linking the quotation to the paragraph of regular context, as in this example:

The greater degree of division of labor in the manufacturing processes employed in this country has lessened the need for specific job training. In fact, Benton says:

A recent survey indicated that millions of the tasks performed by workers can be learned on the job. An even more significant finding is that, even taking into consideration the professions, training for 55 per cent of all positions requires but three weeks or less. . . .

Responsibility in quoting another

● It is important to remember that, unless the contrary is clearly stated, the citation of another's opinion or conclusions usually signifies the writer's acceptance of the point of view as also his own. It is wise, therefore, to investigate carefully the grounds for considering the opinion valid. Not infrequently, care in such matters overturns opinions commonly accepted, or reveals important new facts and thus materially alters the conclusions that the investigation in progress finally reaches. It is often dangerous to accept alleged facts, even from high authority, without personal confirmation.

Quotations in term papers

● The rules for quotations hold for term papers, seminar reports, and book reviews, as well as for theses and dissertations. Student writers of term papers tend to use an excessive number of direct quotations, primarily because most of their sources consist of printed matter, whereas in theses original data and researches are more frequently the basis for statements. Paraphrases or digests of source quotations can be used advantageously to break the monotony of direct quotation, but they do not relieve the writer of the responsibility for acknowledging indebtedness for borrowed ideas. Credit to sources must always be duly given, whether the material is paraphrased or quoted word for word.

Many of the pitfalls commonly encountered in writing term papers may be minimized, or entirely avoided, if the student will read widely on the topic at hand, taking copious notes as he does so; will carefully digest what he has read, in order to have ideas of his own about his topic, as well as an accumulation of ideas borrowed from his reading; will logically outline the steps he intends to follow in presenting his case; and will give careful attention to how he phrases his statements.

The usual purpose of the term paper is to give the student experience in research and writing. The task of preparing a good paper is seldom easy. If, however, the serious student will exert the effort necessary to produce a worth-while product, he will find that, in addition to this immediate result, he will have developed skill in thinking and in handling the ideas of others to bolster his original concepts.

4 | FOOTNOTE AND BIBLIO-
GRAPHICAL REFERENCES

THE STANDARDS OF SCHOLARSHIP require that all source material be acknowledged by the writer, not merely as a matter of common honesty but also as a validation of his work. The authority or source for every fact, opinion, or conclusion quoted, literally or otherwise, must be given. Credit for ideas or statements that have been taken from any publication, lecture, interview, or other source should be given in the text or footnotes, or both. Giving credit for borrowed ideas is as necessary as an acknowledgment for the use of the exact words, symbols, or other form of expression used by the one from whom the idea came.

I. FOOTNOTES

Although the footnotes in a thesis are most likely to be citations of sources, they may also be used to support or supplement content in other ways. Before making a footnote, one should carefully consider whether the matter does not belong in the text, where there is maximum emphasis on the ideas that are being presented to the reader. Against this possibility, however, one should weigh the danger of distracting the reader's attention by the introduction of an irrelevant item. Citations of names, authors, and titles of publications belong unmistakably in footnotes, except when the name of the author or the title of a publication is an essential part of the discussion. If the identity of the authority is of no particular consequence to the reader in following the thought, such phrases as "it is held by one writer" or "according to a prominent authority" may be used in the text and the source of the information indicated in the footnote.

The purposes of footnotes, detailed below, really indicate when a footnote is permissible or needed; but this general rule regarding the use of footnotes must at all times be carefully observed: *Each footnote must in practice be required to justify its existence.*

Purposes of footnote references

● Footnotes have four chief purposes:

1. *To establish the validity of evidence.* All important statements of fact that are not common knowledge must be supported by the presentation of evidence for their validity. This may be done in the text, in the footnotes, or in both. Reference is given in footnotes to the place where such evidence may be found, thus providing the means for verification of the writer's statements and for extension of the inquiry beyond the scope of the thesis.

2. *To acknowledge indebtedness.* A footnote should be supplied for each important statement of fact, for each quotation, and for each conclusion or inference borrowed from another writer. Not only must the source of every direct quotation be given, but a citation is just as necessary when a passage is paraphrased or its substance presented.

Common facts of general knowledge, which every intelligent reader may be assumed to know, require no citation, but even in such a case a footnote reference is necessary if an exact quotation is used.

3. *To amplify the discussion beyond the point permissible in the text.* The general principle governing the distinction between materials for the text and those for the footnotes is that the movement of the text should not be clogged by references and illustrations. Content footnotes may be used to discuss or amplify points that cannot be discussed in the body of the text without complicating the presentation. Footnotes should relieve the text of matter that interrupts its flow and that tends to lessen its interest, such as technical discussions, incidental comments, corollary materials, and additional information upon topics mentioned in the text. Explanatory material of a less important nature, such as reconciliation of conflicting views, may also be placed in footnotes rather than in the text.

The use of footnotes for this purpose calls for considerable discretion. Care should be taken not to lose force by transferring valuable and significant facts to the footnotes, since all very important material should be included in the text. Distinctly unimportant and irrelevant material should not be preserved in the footnotes or elsewhere but should be omitted from the thesis.

4. *To provide cross-reference to various parts of the thesis.* Reference to materials appearing in the appendix, or appendixes, or in earlier or later portions of the manuscript, may, in the interest of clarity, be made in the footnotes.

Footnote superscripts or indexes

● A footnote reference is indicated by placing an index number — that is, a raised, or superscript, numeral — immediately after the end of the statement, or the mark of punctuation ending the material, for which the reference is given. No space intervenes between the word, or the mark of punctuation, and the superscript that follows it. No terminal punctuation is used after the superscript numeral, either in the text or in a footnote.

In order to avoid interrupting the attention of the reader, the superscript for a footnote reference is best placed at the end of a sentence, provided there is no likelihood of confusion. The index number may follow an author's name or a particular title; but if there is a directly quoted or a paraphrased excerpt, the number must appear at the end of the quotation.

Recommended practice is for footnote references to be numbered consecutively for each chapter. In some few institutions, they are required to be numbered continuously throughout the thesis.

Theses containing numerous mathematical or scientific formulas may well use asterisks, daggers, and other symbols in place of superscript numerals or lower-case letters, which might be mistaken as part of the formula.

Special attention is given to footnote superscripts for tabular materials on page 22.

Entries specifically illustrating these matters of form for footnotes may be seen in the sample pages in the Appendix, pages 86 to 88.

For directions as to the proper amount of material that may be placed on a page, including space allowance for and arrangement of footnotes, see Chapter 6.

Methods of inserting footnotes

● Several methods of inserting footnote citations are in use at the present time, each with its special functions, its advantages, and its disadvantages. Only two of these will be described in this manual, since they are the ones accepted in thesis work by the majority of institutions that confer advanced degrees.

The first method consists in inserting the footnote immediately following the reference to it. When this is done, the footnote is separated from the text by one unbroken line above and one below it, as in the following illustration:

to be pursued to turn travel pictures into cash is described

by Forman in his most recent publication.[1] Very little is

---

[1]Harrison Forman, How to Make Money with Your Camera
(New York: McGraw-Hill Book Company, 1952), pp. 115-36.

---

told about the mechanical details of camera operation, for

it is assumed that those who are ready to undertake the sale

The second method is that of collecting at the bottom of any given page all the footnotes for citations made on that page. This most nearly approximates the form in which printed materials appear, and it is the method to be used in preparing a thesis that, in all probability, will not be published. Each footnote should be indented as a paragraph and single-spaced. When two or more footnotes appear at the bottom of any page, a double space should be allowed between them. In numbering the footnotes, the series should begin anew with each chapter (the common method) or else run consecutively throughout the thesis as a whole; it should not start over again on each page.

Footnotes at the bottom of the page are separated from the text by a line one and one-half inches long (fifteen Pica spaces on a typewriter or eighteen Elite spaces), drawn from the left-hand margin toward the center of the page and one double space below the last line of text on that page.

This second method of inserting footnotes is the one used in this manual, and discussions relating to footnotes will be based on it.

In each chapter, the first reference to any source should be complete, since, as in the case of scientific works, it frequently happens that single chapters of a thesis are published. Later references in that chapter need not give such complete data. (See pages 39 to 41.) *Every source cited in a footnote must appear in the bibliography.*

Multiple footnotes • When a citation refers to two or more sources, all may be referred to in a single footnote, with each reference separated from the others by a semicolon, as in the following illustration:

---

[2]Harry J. Baker, Introduction to Exceptional Children
(New York: The Macmillan Company, 1944), pp. 256-72; K. P.
Bradway, "Social Competence of Exceptional Children," Journal of Exceptional Children, 4:38-42, April, 1937 [or IV
(April, 1937), 38-42]; and A. F. Tredgold, Mental Deficiency
(6th ed.; Baltimore: The Williams and Wilkins Company,
1937), p. 386.

Numerous short footnotes • Because of the unbalanced appearance of a typed page with many short footnotes at the bottom, each separated from the other by a double space, it is permissible to place several such short entries on one line, with a minimum of three intervening spaces between the end of one note and the beginning of another, *if all entries on any given line are complete on that line.* It is not acceptable to start an entry on one line and end it on another, or even to make a full, short entry on a line with a footnote begun on a previous line.

Right: ³Johnson, op. cit., pp. 96-99.   ⁴Ibid., pp. 180-89.
Wrong: ⁵Blackstone, op. cit., p. 240.   ⁶George Bilainkin,
Tito (New York: Philosophical Library, Inc., 1950), p. 52.

Wrong: ⁷Frank Gibney, Five Gentlemen of Japan (New York:
Farrar, Straus and Young, 1953), p. 63.   ⁸Ibid., p. 73.

Continued footnotes

• There are occasions when it is necessary to start a footnote on a page that does not have ample space for it to be included in its entirety. When this happens, the footnote should be broken in the middle of a sentence (to do so at the end of a complete sentence might not indicate to the reader that there is more to it) and the remainder carried over to the bottom of the next page under the separation line and preceding any footnotes on that page. When this is done, it is not necessary to call special attention to the fact that the footnote is continued on the next page.

Footnotes to tables and Figures

• A footnote appended to a table or a Figure should be placed one single space below it but not separated from it by a dividing line. Each footnote should be single-spaced if it occupies more than one line, with the first line indented the usual number of spaces — seven. If a table or a Figure has more than one footnote, a double space intervenes between the last line of one footnote and the first line of the next.

In tables and Figures, footnote superscripts should be lower-case letters or symbols (such as the asterisk, dagger, etc.) rather than Arabic numerals. The same series of superscripts should be repeated for each table or Figure; the sequence is not continued consecutively throughout the chapter or thesis, as for the text footnotes.

Footnotes in term papers

• Footnotes are not only an apparatus of scholarship. They also occur in newspapers and in such widely read popular publications as *The Reader's Digest* and *Time*. Because of this widespread occurrence, there is no reason why even the high-school student should not become thoroughly familiar with footnotes and skilled in using them. As a general rule, one reason for requiring term papers and seminar reports is to instruct the uninitiated in proper research and reporting techniques.

The purposes of footnotes and the when and why of using them are the same for theses, dissertations, seminar and committee reports, and term papers.

Because a term paper is shorter and less formal than a thesis, it is possible that the functions of footnotes and bibliography may be merged, thus resulting in one of the following situations: (1) footnotes so complete with regard to facts of publication that a bibliography is not absolutely required; or (2) a bibliography listing all references cited in such complete form that the facts of publication may be omitted from the footnotes. This latter plan, in fact, is applied to graduate theses in many reputable institutions of higher learning. Its use is a question of style and not of being right or wrong. The student should ascertain from his instructor exactly the plan to be followed and then use this manual as a guide in the arrangement of details.

The practice of inserting a footnote where it is needed and of including the essential data in the right order is easily developed. The acquisition of this habit should be an anticipated outcome of the effort required to prepare term papers and other academic reports.

II. BIBLIOGRAPHY

A bibliography is a formal list of materials relating to a particular subject. In a thesis, it must include all the references cited by the student and any others he believes are particularly pertinent to his work.

Distinction between footnote and bibliographical entries

● The function of the bibliography should be clearly distinguished from that of the footnotes. The latter are used to cite authority for specific statements; they designate the exact place where the authoritative utterance is located. The bibliography gives certain necessary descriptive details for the works, as wholes, in which the data cited in footnotes are to be found. The bibliography gives its description once for all, whereas a footnote supports a specific statement by a particular citation. These functions do not fully overlap; hence, a thesis should always include a formal bibliography, and strictly bibliographical matter (complete description of publications) may be limited in the footnotes, or omitted from them entirely. If an article is prepared for publication in a journal, the bibliography is often dispensed with, in which case complete bibliographical data should be included in the footnotes.

The bibliography is complementary to the footnotes as well as to the thesis as a whole; if a reader wants to look up a reference that he finds in a footnote, he can turn to the bibliography to find a full description of the work. The importance of the data that each supplies and the relations between them are further illustrated in the Check List of Footnote Forms and Corresponding Bibliographical Entries, pages 104 to 111.

Classification of entries

● To facilitate the use of a bibliography, the references should be classified and grouped, as much as possible, according to their character. For example, books may be listed in one group, periodicals in a second group, and newspapers in still another. When a bibliography is short, containing fewer than twenty-five or thirty titles, such grouping is seldom necessary.

The broad distinction between primary and secondary sources, as they are sometimes called, although often used as a basis of classification, is not entirely satisfactory if there is no further subgrouping of items. Probably no two bibliographies can be classified on exactly the same plan, because the character of the materials and their grouping varies with the subject and the purpose of the thesis. An ideal method for theses in the field of literature is to classify the works into primary and secondary sources, with subdivisions in each. Although sometimes no basis for such a breakdown will appear for the primary sources, it is rare indeed that the list of secondary works will not lend itself to some system of subgrouping. The number and kinds of groups will depend upon the nature of the problem being investigated, the availability of a reference literature, the kinds of references used, and the length of the bibliography.

Selected bibliography

● Rather than have a so-called "complete" bibliography, it is usually better to have a "selected" bibliography. This latter type, especially in the instance of subjects with numerous references, will be more useful to future students than a complete bibliography of all the reading done for the study, which might include good, bad, and mediocre items.

Sometimes the bibliography is extended to embrace works not used directly in writing the thesis, in order to furnish a background for the subject. Such a bibliography is not "complete" but is still "selected."

Irrespective of the basis of selection or the extent of the material included, non-essential works have no place in a thesis bibliography. In any case, however, all literature reviewed or cited by the student in the text of his work must be listed.

Annotated bibliography

● In scholarly works, the bibliography is often annotated, that is, each entry is followed by a comment indicating its value and its relationship to the subject. Annotated bibliographies are often required in prize competitions. Since an annotation relates the reference to the theme of the study, obviously an annotated bibliography is more useful to the reader than one which is not annotated. Also, the requirement that each entry be annotated tends to prevent the "padding" of bibliographies — an unscholarly but not uncommon practice.

The annotation should be brief and related pointedly to the subject investigated. It should not be filled with platitudes, flattery, or meaningless statements. At its best, it will consist of a brief exposition of the nature and content of the work, its relationship to the present study, and, perhaps, any use that may be made of it by the reader.

The student can save himself from needless expenditure of time and energy by gathering the complete data needed for each entry in the bibliography at the time the work is consulted during the course of the investigation. Comments in the form of brief notes made at that time may readily be phrased into annotations for the bibliography.

The entire annotation is aligned with the four-space indention, single-spaced, and with only a single space between the bibliographical entry and the annotation. There is a double space between the end of the annotation and the beginning of the following entry. This form is used in the illustrations on page 103.

Form of bibliographical entries

● The entries in the bibliography are arranged in an underhung, single-spaced form. Each entry begins flush with the left-hand margin, and the second and ensuing lines, if any, are indented four spaces.

Within an unclassified bibliography, or within the groupings of a classified bibliography, it is appropriate to alphabetize the works by surname of author, or by initial letter of title in the case of an anonymous or unknown author.

When there are two or more works by the same author, repetition of his name may be avoided by substituting an unbroken line seven spaces in length. This begins flush with the left-hand margin and is followed by a period. All listings for any author are further alphabetized under his name, but publications of which he is co-author follow *after* those of which he is sole author, as in the following list:

Chase, Stuart. Government in Business. New York: The
    Macmillan Company, 1935. 296 pp. [Or, Pp. ix+296;
    or the number of pages may be omitted.]
    One of the first works by a major economist openly
    advocating considerable control of business by govern-
    ment.

_____. A New Deal. New York: The Macmillan Company,
    1932. 257 pp. [Or, Pp. vi+257; or the number of pages
    may be omitted.]
    A pre-Roosevelt plea for a new economic policy on
    the part of the Government.

_____. The Tyranny of Words. New York: Harcourt, Brace
    and Company, 1938. 396 pp. [Or, Pp. viii+396; or the
    number of pages may be omitted.]
    A standard book in the field of semantics, with many
    of the illustrations drawn from the field of economics.

_____, and Marian Tyler. Mexico: A Study of Two Americas.
    New York: The Macmillan Company, 1931. 269 pp. [Or,
    Pp. iv+269; or the number of pages may be omitted.]
    A portrayal of culture patterns in a Mexican city and
    a Mexican village, based on technological developments.

III. FORMS OF ENTRIES

Books

● The items that are indispensable to a complete book reference are enumerated and discussed below, in the order of their appearance:

1. *The name of the author*, editor, compiler, or translator stands first and includes the given name and/or initials in the form appearing on the title-page of the book. The natural order of given name followed by surname may be used in the footnotes, where alphabetization is unnecessary; but the necessity for arranging bibliographical entries in alphabetical order makes it desirable that the surname there appear first. The given name may be dropped after this first occurrence, if no misunderstanding will result, for example, when used with *op. cit.* and *loc. cit.* (see pages 39 to 41). The two forms are shown in the following illustrations, the first of which, in each case, is for the footnote:

[1]John C. Almack, Research and Thesis Writing (Boston: Houghton Mifflin Company, 1930), p. 218.

This same entry would appear in the thesis bibliography thus:

Almack, John C. Research and Thesis Writing. Boston: Houghton Mifflin Company, 1930. 310 pp. [Or, Pp. vii+ 310; or omit number of pages.]

In certain scientific fields, footnote form calls for the surname to precede the given name, as in the bibliography.

When a book has two or three authors, all of their names are listed. The usual order of given names preceding surnames is correct for footnotes; for the bibliography, the same scheme is followed except in the instance of the first-named author, where the surname comes before the given name.

If the title-page lists more than three authors, only that of the first, followed by the abbreviation *et al.*, or the English phrase "and others," is used. The following footnote entries are for three authors and more than three authors, respectively:

[2]Witt Bowden, Michael Karpovich, and Abbott Payson Usher, An Economic History of Europe Since 1750 (New York: American Book Company, 1937), p. 422.

[3]Charles H. Johnston and others [or, et al.], The Modern High School (New York: Charles Scribner's Sons, 1914), pp. 603-14.

The correct bibliographical entries for the above references are as follows:

Bowden, Witt, Michael Karpovich, and Abbott Payson Usher. An Economic History of Europe Since 1750. New York: American Book Company, 1937. 948 pp.

Johnston, Charles H., and others [or, et al.]. The Modern High School. New York: Charles Scribner's Sons, 1914. 847 pp.

If the name is that of an editor, compiler, or translator, such a notation, enclosed by parentheses, follows the name. Under these conditions, the following examples represent the correct footnote and bibliographical forms, respectively:

```
     4C. O. Sylvester Mawson (ed.), Roget's Interna-
tional Thesaurus of English Words and Phrases (New York:
Thomas Y. Crowell Company, 1925), p. 314.

Mawson, C. O. Sylvester (ed.).  Roget's International
     Thesaurus of English Words and Phrases.  New York:
     Thomas Y. Crowell Company, 1925.  741 pp.
```

In the case of an anonymous or unknown author, or where the authorship is not specified, the citation begins immediately with the title of the work, and order of alphabetization is determined by title rather than by author.

2. *The exact title*, taken from the title-page, is then given. In a typewritten manuscript this title is underscored, and in the bibliography it is punctuated at the end by a period. Excessive abbreviation of the title is not in good taste.

3. *The facts of publication* include the edition (if more than one), the volume number, the place of publication, the name of the publisher, and the date of publication or copyright. The examples given show the facts of publication in their proper order.

In the footnote reference, the facts of publication for a book are enclosed in parentheses. These may be omitted after their first citation in any chapter *and may be omitted altogether* if the bibliography lists the work in question, in which case, of course, the data appear there. In general, a footnote should be as concise as the demand for full clarity will permit. Proper abbreviations for second and later citations are given on pages 39 to 41.

The forms "Vol." or "Vols." and "p." or "pp." are generally omitted when both items are included in the same reference, except in cases where the figures might be misunderstood to stand for something else. Since the Roman chapter numeral may be mistaken for a volume reference, a chapter number ordinarily requires the use of the abbreviation "Chap." or, in works of literary research, the Latinized form "Cap." The volume number is given in capital Roman numerals and the page reference in Arabic numerals. The total number of volumes in the work (if more than one) is stated only in the bibliographical entry. Lower-case Roman numerals are used in citing pages in the introductory portions of a book, if they are there so numbered.

The place of publication is entered next. When several offices are listed on the title-page, as in the case of large publishing houses, the first named is usually the editorial office. For large cities, it is not necessary to name the state or country; otherwise, both city and state, or city and country, are necessary. These are separated by a comma, and the latter item is followed by a colon. If no place of publication is given, the bracketed abbreviation [n.p.] ("no place") is used. If the place of publication is supplied by the writer from external sources, it is enclosed in square brackets to indicate that it is interpolated: [London].

The name of the publisher must be copied in exactly the form given on the title-page, as a matter of courtesy, and should be followed by a comma. If the name is not given in the book, the omission is indicated by inserting [n.n.] ("no name"). If the information is interpolated by the writer from external sources, it is inserted within square brackets: [The Smith Company].

The date of the publication or copyright of the book follows the name of the publisher. When there is more than one volume in the edition, the inclusive dates of publication must be given: "1942–48." If the publication is still in progress, this fact is indicated by leaving the second date blank: "1949–   ." If the work cited is a revised edition, the date of the edition used is given. If the date of publication does not appear on the title-page, the copyright date from the following page may be substituted. In the event that that also is missing, the abbreviation [n.d.] ("no date") should be used. If the date of publication is supplied from external sources, it should be enclosed in square brackets: [1861].

⁵Paul Monroe (ed.), A Cyclopedia of Education (New York: The Macmillan Company, 1911), I, 345.

⁶Ibid., II, 16-35.

⁷Ibid., p. vii.

In the bibliography, however, the entry covering all three of these would be:

Monroe, Paul (ed.). A Cyclopedia of Education. 5 vols. New York: The Macmillan Company, 1911.

4. *The page numbers*, followed by a period, are indicated next. In a footnote, the exact page numbers to which reference is made should be shown, unless a whole chapter is cited, in which case either the number or number and title of the chapter (the latter enclosed in quotation marks) will suffice. For example: p. 27. pp. 28–39. Chapter II, "Techniques of Research."

For a bibliographical entry, three styles have general acceptance; the student will have to learn which is suggested, or required, by his department or university. (1) Make no reference to the total number of pages. Few books, other than texts, give this type of information. (2) The total of pages numbered in Arabic numerals, followed by the abbreviation "pp.," for example, 310 pp. (3) The abbreviation "Pp.," then the number of preliminary pages numbered in lower-case Roman numerals, followed by the number of pages in Arabic numerals, for example, Pp. viii + 310. Various specimens in this manual illustrate one or another of all these styles.

Periodical literature ● Some of the data needed for book citations are not required for references to periodical literature. The names of the publishers and the places of publication of current journals are generally known and are easily ascertainable. Moreover, each article is, in a sense, a separate work.

In the bibliography, each article is listed separately under the author's name, with an indication of the issue of the periodical in which it is printed. The bibliographical entry for an article and the footnote first citing it are practically duplicates in both form and substance. Like the corresponding entries for books, they differ in three respects: (1) In the bibliography, the surname precedes the given name, whereas in the footnote reference the given name, or initials, appears first; (2) in the bibliography, a period, rather than a comma, follows the name and initials of the author; and (3) in the footnote, if the reference is to specific pages, only their numbers are indicated, whereas in the bibliography and in footnotes where specific pages are not cited the inclusive pages of the article are given. These points are illustrated in the examples on page 28.

A complete reference for articles in magazines should be in the following form and in the order given:

1. *The name of the author* stands first, followed by a comma in a footnote, a period in a bibliographical entry. The special usages noted in connection with the author item given for book entries, page 25, should be followed in their entirety. When the name of the author is not known, the title of the article appears first in the citation, and the alphabetization in the bibliography is by the first letter in the title rather than by the name of the author.

2. *The title of the article* is given in full, followed by a comma, and is enclosed in quotation marks. The initial letters of all important words are capitalized, as in book titles.

3. *The facts of publication*, including the name of the periodical (underscored) in which the article appears, the volume number in capital Roman numerals, the date of publication (year, month, and day of month, if necessary to make it complete) enclosed in parentheses, and the page number, or numbers, follow in that order.

8William Hard, "The Fight at Niagara," The Reader's Digest, LXIII (August, 1953), 30.

The preceding citation was to only one page of the article. The complete bibliographical entry, using this form, would appear as follows:

Hard, William. "The Fight at Niagara," The Reader's Digest, LXIII (August, 1953), pp. 27-32.

A convenient and compact arrangement for the facts of publication, used by many modern scientific journals and acceptable in theses in some universities, consists in giving the volume number in Arabic numerals, followed without intervening spaces by a colon and the page reference. The month and year of publication, separated by a comma, stand last. The following are examples of footnote and bibliographical entries using this form:

8William Hard, "The Fight at Niagara," The Reader's Digest, 63:30, August, 1953.

Hard, William. "The Fight at Niagara," The Reader's Digest, 63:27-32, August, 1953.

Special forms for the sciences and mathematics

● Because in the general area of the sciences and mathematics special practices with regard to footnote and bibliographical entries have been developed and are in vogue today, this special section dealing with these subjects is included.

As a generalization, it may be said that the science or mathematics student will find one of the three following plans accepted as standard in his school: (1) The thesis will contain footnotes but no bibliography, and all sources considered sufficiently important will be referred to in this way; (2) the thesis will have only a bibliography but no footnotes, each citation in the text will there be listed, and both works specifically referred to and others considered pertinent will be included; or (3) there will be both footnotes and a bibliography, as in other academic fields. The latter plan is being adopted by more and more universities for thesis work.

Even with the matter of footnotes and bibliography (either or both) determined, the student may learn that special forms for entries have been adopted, usually in keeping with one of the three following styles: (1) The science or mathematics department prescribes the same style as is used by other departments, such as English, history, and education; (2) the department stipulates that the style and practices regarding footnotes and bibliography accord with those established by the major professional body, or bodies, in the field; or (3) the department specifies the general usages followed by the editors of the outstanding journals in that field, with only such modifications as are necessary because the work is a thesis and not an article.

Even before starting his library work, the student should ascertain what standards apply to his case, so that the notes he takes in the course of his reading will allow him to meet requirements.

In general, it may be said that if footnotes are to appear in the thesis, whatever the field, the directions given above regarding their justification and insertion (see pages 19 to 22) will apply, as will also the use of shortened forms in second and later references to the same source — *ibid.*, *loc. cit.*, and *op. cit.* (see pages 39–41).

If footnotes are not to be used, in which case each citation will be to some publication listed at the end of the thesis (the list may be called the Bibliography, Literature Cited, or List of References), the custom is to enclose the reference numeral in parentheses on the same line as the text and number the entries correspondingly. The following will illustrate the exact placement of numbers, spacing, and other details.

The text citations:

and while there were differences in the methods used and the

details, Brown (1), Davis (2), and Manley (3) were all in

The bibliographical entries:

1. William Brown, <u>Plane</u> <u>and</u> <u>Spherical</u> <u>Geometry</u>, New York. 1952.

2. Stephen Davis, <u>Algebra</u> <u>for</u> <u>Teachers</u>, Boston, 1950.

3. William Dwight Manley, <u>Applications</u> <u>of</u> <u>Differential</u> <u>Equations</u>, San Francisco, 1951.

The practices above outlined offer two possible variations with regard to listing sources: (1) The citations will occur in the thesis in numerical order, from 1 up, in which case the listed words probably will not be in alphabetical order; or (2) the works cited will be alphabetized and numbered consecutively in the bibliography, and the numbers citing them will not occur in consecutive order in the text. The second of these variations provides a more convenient means of handling several text citations to the same source. The student must ask which is the accepted plan in his institution.

Not only does variation from field to field exist, but even within a given field of scientific specialization there is not always agreement regarding all details of how to present typed materials. In order that the most useful possible directions might be given here, the editors of more than thirty of the major scientific journals of the United States, representing all the major fields of science, were asked to indicate what, in their estimation, constituted most acceptable footnote and bibliographical form of typed matter. Since nearly all responded and cooperated, the specimens given on ensuing pages should carry considerable weight in the preparation of theses in the several fields indicated.

The following are the most commonly recommended styles in the fields listed. In some instances, it was necessary to choose between two recommended forms; in a few, minor adaptations to other directions given in this manual account for the illustration presented. Special attention is called to the tendency to use abbreviations for the titles of journal articles. Several source lists of approved abbreviations will be found in the Bibliography, page 70; others may be available, as time goes on, from the more prominent publications in any given field.

Biology and zoology ● Book reference:

Henesy, G. 1948. Radioactive Indicators. Interscience
   Publishers, Inc., New York.

● Journal references:

Fuller, W. H. and Norman, A. G. 1943. Characteristics of
   some soil cytophages. Jour. Bact. 45:565-572.

Gollsoff, P. S. 1934. The biochemistry of invertebrates
   of the sea. Ecol. Monog., 4:481-490.

Botany ● Book references:

Bower, F. O. 1935. Primitive Land Plants. 658 pp.

Eames, A. J. 1936. Morphology of Vascular Plants. Lower
   groups. 433 pp.

Zobell, C. E. 1946. Marine Microbiology. 208 pp.

● Journal references (note that letters are used to indicate more than one work by
   an author in a single year, and that listing is by *date* and not by title):

Schanderl, H. 1942a. Vergleichende Untersuchungen über den
   Stickstoffhaushalt von Leguminosen unter Nechellegum-
   inosen. Ber. Deut. Bot. Gaz. 60:85-93.

_____ 1942b. Assimilation of elemental nitrogen of
   the air by yeast symbionts of Rhagum inquisitor. Zeit.
   Morphol. Okol. Tiere 38:526-533.

_____ 1943. The N content of leguminous and non-
   leguminous plants. Planta 33:424-457.

Chemistry ● Book reference:

[9]Linus Pauling, "The Nature of the Chemical Bond,"
Cornell University Press, Ithaca, New York, 1940, p. 123.

● Journal references:

[10]W. L. Jolly, Chem. Revs., 50, 351 (1952).

[11]S. Winstein and R. E. Buckles, J. Am. Chem. Soc.,
64, 2780 (1942).

Geography and geology ● Book references:

Gillespie, C. C. (1951) Genesis and Geology, Harvard
   University Press, Cambridge.

Pettijohn, F. J. (1949) Sedimentary Rocks, Harper and
   Brothers, New York.

● Journal references (note method of indicating author or authors of more than one work):

Hudson, R. G. S. (1942) An upper Viséan zaphrentoid fauna from the Yoredale beds of northwest Yorkshire: Yorkshire Geol. Soc. Proc., vol. 25, pp. 101-126, pls. 9-12.

———— and Turner, J. S. (1933a) Early and mid-Carboniferous earth movements in Great Britain: Leeds Philos. Soc. Proc., vol. 2, pp. 455-466, charts.

———— ——— ———— (1933b) Correlation of Dinantian and Namurian in western Europe: ibid., pp. 467-482.

Mathematics
● Book references:

[12]Gilbert Ames Bliss, Mathematics for Exterior Ballistics, New York, 1944, pp. 23-36.

[13]Tibor Rado, Subharmonic Functions, Berlin, 1944.

● Journal references:

[14]O. J. Ramler, Quadratic and cubic equations, American Mathematical Monthly, vol. 50 (1943), pp. 507-509.

[15]D. V. Widder, Inversion formulas for convolution transforms, Duke Mathematical Journal, vol. 14 (1947), pp. 217-249.

Physics
● Book references:

[16]L. Pauling and E. B. Wilson, Introduction to Quantum Mechanics (McGraw-Hill Book Company, Inc., New York, 1935), p. 344.

[17]L. Diesendruck, dissertation, The Johns Hopkins University, 1950.

● Journal references:

[18]M. Kac and J. C. Ward, Phys. Rev. 88, 1332 (1952).

[19]J. Kirkwood, J. Chem. Phys. 6, 70 (1938).

Psychology
● Book reference:

Jefferds, C. V., Jr. The psychology of industrial unrest. New York: McGraw-Hill, 1951.

● Journal references:

Archer, P. W. The tactile perception of roughness. Amer. J. Psychol., 1950, 63, 365-373.

Entries of essays ● References to essays or articles in annuals, university studies, composite books, and similar volumes resemble book entries in some ways and article entries in others. The title of the essay is enclosed in quotation marks, and the title of the volume is underscored. Page citations are necessary, because the study does not fill the entire volume. Up to this point the entry resembles that for a periodical article. However, the place and date of publication of the volume in which the essay appears must also be given as in a book entry. The proper forms for footnote and bibliographical references, respectively, are shown below:

[20]H. R. Wagner, "Hispanic Americana in the John Carter Brown Library," Essays Honoring Lawrence C. Wroth (Portland, Me.: Anthoensen Press, 1951), pp. 91-96.

Wagner, H. R. "Hispanic Americana in the John Carter Brown Library," Essays Honoring Lawrence C. Wroth. Portland, Me.: Anthoensen Press, 1951. Pp. 72-108.

Parts of a series ● References to books in a series should cite the specific volume used and also indicate its place in the series. Both footnote and bibliographical entries describe the volume cited in its relation to the whole series. If the volumes of the series are organic parts of the whole, the bibliography should contain, in addition to the description of the particular volume cited, an entry describing the series as a whole. In this case, the title of the series in which the book appears, as well as the title of the individual volume, must be underscored. The proper forms for the footnote and the two necessary bibliographical entries are shown below:

[21]Max Farrand, The Fathers of the Constitution (Vol. XIII of The Chronicles of America Series, ed. Allen Johnson. 50 vols.; New Haven: Yale University Press, 1918-21), p. 163.

Farrand, Max. The Fathers of the Constitution. Vol. XIII of The Chronicles of America Series. Edited by Allen Johnson. 50 vols. New Haven: Yale University Press, 1918-21.

Johnson, Allen (ed.). The Chronicles of America Series. 50 vols. New Haven: Yale University Press, 1918-21.

If the volume cited is an independent study and is merely numbered in a series, no separate entry for the series is needed in the bibliography, but the publisher and place of publication of the individual volume should be given in connection with the volume entry in both bibliography and footnote references, as is shown below:

[22]Ira B. Cross, Stuart Daggett, and Carl C. Plehn, The Dependent Aged in San Francisco (University of California Publications in Economics, Vol. V, No. 1. Berkeley, California: University of California Press, 1928), p. 110.

Cross, Ira B., Stuart Daggett, and Carl C. Plehn, The Dependent Aged in San Francisco. University of California Publications in Economics, Vol. V, No. 1. Berkeley, California: University of California Press, 1928.

Publications of the Government, learned societies, and other organizations

❧ In recent years, there has been a tremendous increase in the number of publications made available by the United States Government and by various organizations interested in research and publication. Many of these are important to the writer of a thesis. The fact that most of them are not issued by regular publishing houses and bear the name of an organization not thought of as engaged in the publishing business may present some difficulties in footnote and bibliographical citation.

There are no absolute rules of form for listing these documents in footnotes and bibliographies, but the following list will serve as a guide to the student faced with the task of preparing a thesis in which they have been used:

1. An essay or article in a report, an annual, or a study that does not fill the entire volume should be treated as a periodical article, that is to say, its title is enclosed in quotes and the title of the volume is underscored.

2. A report or an investigation that occupies an entire volume, with its title on the title-page, should be treated as a book and the title underscored in the citation. An individual or a sponsoring organization may be named author; or the book may be cited as without an author (the report of some group) and the work alphabetized by title of publication.

3. A citation to a publication that is part of a series, such as a yearbook of an association or part of a series in some special field published by a university, should show enough of the facts of the relationship so that those who know the field may quickly place the work.

4. If these data still do not give enough information for a complete entry, the thesis writer should include enough additional facts of publication, at least in the bibliography, to enable an interested party to locate the work. For example, the place where even well-known organizations have their headquarters is not always known; or the place of publication may be different from the place where the group or institution sponsoring the study is based. The writer of a thesis is morally obligated to make it possible for readers to examine the sources that he cites.

Some colleges require complete facts of publication to appear in the footnotes; others accept a much abbreviated form; but all insist that full facts of publication be given in bibliographical entries. The following illustrations will help the student who is working with this type of material. Footnotes might be as follows:

[23]G. M. Wilson, "A Survey of the Social and Business Use of Arithmetic," Second Report of the Committee on Minimal Essentials in Elementary School Subjects, Sixteenth Yearbook of the National Society for the Study of Education, Part I (Bloomington, Illinois: Public School Publishing Company, 1917), pp. 20-22.

[24]American Library Association, Personnel Organization and Procedure, A Report Prepared by the Board on Personnel Administration (Chicago: American Library Association, 1952), p. 17.

[25]Personnel Organization and Procedure, A Report Prepared by the Board on Personnel Administration (Chicago: American Library Association, 1952), p. 17.

[26]Vincent B. Phelan, Care and Repair of the House, National Bureau of Standards, United States Department of Commerce, Circular 489 (Washington: Government Printing Office, 1950), pp. 41-79.

[27]United States Bureau of the Census, Seventeenth Census of the United States: 1950. Population, Vol. II (Washington: Government Printing Office, 1952), p. 33.

In the bibliography, these citations would appear as follows:

Wilson, G. M. "A Survey of the Social and Business Uses of Arithmetic," Second Report of the Committee on Minimal Essentials in Elementary School Subjects, pp. 2-22. Sixteenth Yearbook of the National Society for the Study of Education, Part I. Bloomington, Illinois: Public School Publishing Company, 1917.

American Library Association. Personnel Organization and Procedure. A Report Prepared by the Board on Personnel Administration. Chicago: American Library Association, 1952.

Personnel Organization and Procedure. A Report Prepared by the Board on Personnel Administration. Chicago: American Library Association, 1952.

Phelan, Vincent B. Care and Repair of the House. National Bureau of Standards, United States Department of Commerce, Circular 489. Washington: Government Printing Office, 1950.

United States Bureau of the Census. Seventeenth Census of the United States: 1950. Population, Vol. II. Washington: Government Printing Office, 1952.

Articles in encyclopedias

● References to encyclopedia articles follow the general form for periodical articles. Between the name of the encyclopedia and the number of the volume containing the material, the particular edition should be given for purposes of identification. The following entries exemplify these points:

[28]William Spry, "Homestead and Exemption Laws," Encyclopaedia Britannica (14th ed.), XI, 705.

Spry, William. "Homestead and Exemption Laws," Encyclopaedia Britannica (14th ed.), XI, 702-16.

Accumulated manuscripts and documents

● Manuscripts and other documents are best designated according to the manner in which they are stored or arranged in the depository that holds them. The local system of designations should be studied and followed in detail. Usually the citation must include both the number of the item and the collection in which it will be found. The name of the city or institution where the collection is housed may be necessary, especially with the less-well-known depositories.

[29]Sam Houston Papers (MSS in the Garcia Library, University of Texas), Vol. IV, No. 19.

[30]British Museum, Harleian MSS, 5103, fol. 23.

When a collection of documents is published in book form, its title is underscored and the facts of publication are given, like those for any other book, as in the following illustration:

[31]Letter from George Washington to Alexander Hamilton, July 10, 1787, in Max Farrand (ed.), The Records of the Federal Convention of 1787 (New Haven: Yale University Press, 1911-37), III, 56-57.

Miscellaneous unpublished materials

● With unpublished materials, the title of the work is enclosed in quotation marks, enough about the source is given to enable another to trace it, and nothing is underscored. If the reference is to a paper read before some gathering, the name of the group and the date of the meeting should be stated.

[32]Julian C. Aldrich, "How to Construct and Use a Resource Unit" (New York: Joint Council on Economic Education, 1951), p. 7. (Mimeographed.)

[33]Harold C. Holland, "Dynamics: Some New Perspectives" (paper read at the National Science Laboratory, Northtown, New Jersey, May 11, 1953).

References to theses and dissertations

● In referring to a thesis, it is usually sufficient to give the name of the author, the title of the thesis, the university at which the degree was taken, and the year in which it was granted. The following is the accepted form for a citation of this kind:

[34]Frank L. James, "An Analysis of the Application of Certain Relief Measures in Los Angeles" (unpublished Master's thesis, The University of Southern California, Los Angeles, 1952), p. 112.

In the bibliography, this work would be entered as follows:

James, Frank L. "An Analysis of the Application of Certain Relief Measures in Los Angeles." Unpublished Master's thesis, The University of Southern California, Los Angeles, 1952.

Entries for newspapers

● In references to newspapers, the name of the paper as it is printed on the first page of the paper is the title underscored. If the name of the paper does not indicate its place of publication, the name of the city or the names of both city and state must be interpolated in square brackets. The date of the issue in which the cited article appears must be given.

Page and column references are useful in citing newspapers, but they are often omitted. Editorials or other special classes of items in newspapers should be distinguished.

[35]Editorial in the Los Angeles Times, June 3, 1952.

[36]Associated Press dispatch, The Albuquerque [New Mexico] Tribune, February 17, 1953.

[37]Chicago Tribune, May 7, 1952, p. 8.

[38]Dallas Morning News, December 6, 1953, Part II,
p. 44, col. 2.

A signed article in a special section, such as a magazine section or a literary supplement, is treated like a periodical article:

[39]John Lehmann, "T. S. Eliot Talks About Himself
and the Drive to Create," The New York Times Book Review,
November 29, 1953, pp. 5, 44.

Newspaper items are not listed separately in the bibliography, as are periodical articles, but they are treated like individual items in a collection of documents: the newspaper file is described, either *in toto* or for the period of time (inclusive dates) for which it proved useful. The division of the bibliography devoted to current newspapers may list them merely by name, with any necessary indications of the town or state where published, for example:

The Boston Herald, January, 1942-June, 1953.

Legal and legislative references

● Theses in law and political science require frequent reference to laws, court cases, and the acts of legislative bodies, especially Congress.

While there is not absolute agreement on the style to be used in law citations, they are usually very condensed, even if no further information is contained in the bibliography. Little confusion can result, since the reference forms are more or less standardized and are well known. The following elements are usually included, in the order listed: volume or section, journal, page number, date in parentheses (if necessary, the jurisdiction precedes the date within the parentheses). Examples follow:

[40]Winter v. New York, 333 U.S. 507 (1948).

[41]Dabney v. Chase National Bank, 196 F. 2d, 668
(2d Cir. 1952).

[42]60 Stat. 801 (1950), 50 U.S.C.A. §2092 (Supp.,
1952).

[43]Jones v. Robinson, 3 Abramson 263 (Tenn., 1869).

[44]Rev. Stat. Wisconsin, 1952, Sec. 76.33.

[45]George J. Johnson, "The Present Status of Multiple
Taxation," 46 Harvard Law Review 327 (1948).

It will be noted that the total number of pages is not given. When the citation is to the case as a whole, only the number of the first page is listed; when reference is to a specific point within the case, such as a principle, the numbers of the first page *and* the page containing the cited material, separated by a comma, are given. The following references are to entire cases:

[46]Wheaton v. Peters, 8 Pet. 591 (U.S., 1934).

[47]15 Univ. of Chi. L. Rev. 1 (1947).

If only page 603 in the first case and page 9 in the second were to be cited, the footnotes would take the following form:

[48]Wheaton v. Peters, 8 Pet. 591, 603 (U.S., 1934).

[49]15 Univ. of Chi. L. Rev. 1, 9 (1947).

References to British statutes include regnal year in Arabic numerals, name of the sovereign, comma, lower-case "c" (legal abbreviation for chapter), and the chapter number in Arabic numerals:

[50]Great Britain Statutes at Large, 8 Anne, c. 22.

[51]Amended L. R. Statutes, 1918, 8 George V, c. 1.

Citations of legislative acts must show the body from which the law emanates. In the case of the United States Congress, the standard abbreviations H. R. (House of Representatives) and Sen. (Senate) usually suffice. For example:

[52]United States Department of Commerce, United States Department of Commerce Publications (Washington: Government Printing Office, 1952), p. 633.

[53]United States Congress, Senate, Committee on the Judiciary, Federal Construction Contract Act, Hearings before Subcommittee, 82d Congress, 2d Session, on S. 2907, April 29-June 3, 1952 (Washington: Government Printing Office, 1952), p. 286. [The abbreviations U.S., Cong., and Sess. are often permissible.]

Entries for labor-union documents

● Recent developments in the field of industrial and labor relations make necessary rather frequent reference to labor-management agreements, convention proceedings, union constitutions, arbitration awards, and similar documents. In the past, there has been little uniformity in the style of footnote and bibliographical entries for papers of this kind. Little difficulty will be experienced in preparing the entry so that the reader can understand it and locate the document if the following items are included: (1) The name of the union, inverted to the key word. The correct guide for this inversion is the Bureau of Labor Statistics *Directory of Labor Unions in the United States;* (2) the title of the document, including date (both effective and expiration dates, if applicable); (3) the facts of publication, if any; and (4) the page reference. The following footnote forms exemplify these rules:

[54]Communications Association, American, CIO, Local 40, and the Western Union Telegraph Company, Agreement between, April 1, 1948-April 1, 1949, p. 32.

[55]Longshoremen's and Warehousemen's Union, International, CIO, Proceedings of the Seventh Biennial Convention of San Francisco, April 7 to April 11, 1947 (San Francisco: Trade Pressroom), p. 83.

[56]Stone Cutters Association of North America, Journeymen, Constitution and By-Laws, 1926, p. 4.

In the bibliography, these entries would take the following form:

Communications Association, American, CIO, Local 40, and the Western Union Telegraph Company, Agreement between, April 1, 1948-April 1, 1949. 57 pp.

Longshoremen's and Warehousemen's Union, International, CIO. Proceedings of the Seventh Biennial Convention of San Francisco, April 7 to April 11, 1947. San Francisco: Trade Pressroom. 364 pp.

Stone Cutters Association of North America. Journeymen. Constitution and By-Laws. 1926. 51 pp.

Citing oral discourse ● It is perfectly acceptable, often necessary, to use ideas that have been heard rather than read, if the precautions indicated on page 14 are observed. A bibliographical entry for what was heard is not necessary, but the following is the correct form for the footnote citation:

[57]Statement by John Dewey, personal interview.

[58]Opinion expressed by Dr. James Robertson at a Rotary Club luncheon, New York City, August 19, 1953.

[59]Commencement address, Robert College, Istanbul, Turkey, June 3, 1951.

Documentation of social research ● Many sources of data in the field of the social sciences cannot be listed in the same manner as books and articles. The following suggestions regarding the proper methods of documenting these nonlibrary sources were prepared by Case and should be followed by students who are working with materials not easily listed:

Students engaged in writing up the results of social research in the field are hampered by a distinct gap in the current technique of documentation. This applies equally to footnotes in the report itself and to the formal bibliography often appended to such writings. There is present in such cases a notable inability on the part of the student to marshal the sources of information actually employed in the field study, principally because of the fact that all the manuals for thesis writing are modeled after the traditional practice, which makes no provision for the listing of those sources which are predominant in sociological research. The pattern now in vogue was set originally by history and is dominated by the library type of research. This takes no account of anything but printed or written accounts of events already past, and these it divides into "primary" and "secondary" sources, without recognition of the fact that frequently the "primary sources" for field work in the social sciences are not printed pages of any sort at all, but human beings in their actual social relations here and now.

For these reasons it is suggested that preliminary steps should be taken toward the adoption of a uniform method of documentation in the social sciences, somewhat as follows:

1. To the traditional "Bibliography" there should be appended a supplementary list with its own caption, "Other Sources," in deference to the fact that the word bibliography cannot be stretched to include anything but books without doing violence to its etymology.

2. Under this supplementary list should be included the following categories, namely, (1) Case Records; (2) Manuscript Journals (or Diaries if preferred); (3) Personal Correspondence of the Author; (4) Interviews and Life Histories; (5) Observations (or Field Notes, if preferred) of the Author.

3. In the footnotes of the main text the same terms should be used with the necessary elaboration, such as "Case Record No. 123, County Welfare Association, Los Angeles County, California"; or "Personal Correspondence of the Author, letter from John Doe, Jan. 1, 1933."

The present writer ventures to suggest this plan tentatively, after examination of many sociological research works recently published, and upon consultation with his colleagues in the Department of Sociology, The University of Southern California. In addition to the five categories listed above, some writers use the form "Document No. 123." This is very convenient in cases where one does not wish to specify too closely, but carries with it an all-inclusive vagueness which makes it a sort of covering title for all the other sources named above. For this reason it is not specified here, but recognized as the practice of excellent authorities.[1]

IV. SPECIAL FORMS OF FOOTNOTE REFERENCES

This section deals with certain special words and abbreviations that often occur in footnotes, and occasionally in bibliographies. Many of these special forms of reference involve Latin words or words of Latin origin, and they are part of the tradition of scholarly research and writing. No attempt is made to give an exhaustive list; only the more commonly used terms are considered here.

The guiding consideration, in deciding whether or not to use one of these special forms, should be *brevity* and *clarity*. When they will save the reader's time and help him to understand better, they should be used; when they will merely waste his time or confuse him, some substitute should be found. In other words, they are devices to employ not primarily because they are scholarly, but because they are useful. Constant use of uncommon forms of citation is not necessarily an evidence of scholarship — it may indicate an unwarranted intellectual snobbishness.

Ibid.

• In consecutive references to the same source, the Latin abbreviation *ibid.* (for *ibidem*, "the same") is used to avoid repetition of as much of the preceding citation as is unchanged. If the page number is different, it must follow the abbreviation. In the typed form, the abbreviation *ibid.* must be underlined to indicate italics.

```
60Jon Kimche, Seven Fallen Pillars (London: Secker
and Warburg, 1950), p. 130.

  61Ibid. [This refers to page 130, not to any other.]

  62Ibid., pp. 219-20. [This still refers to Kimche,
                       but to pages 219-20.]
```

---

[1] Clarence Marsh Case, "Note on the Documentation of Social Research," *Sociology and Social Research*, XVII (March–April, 1933), 396–97.

Since *ibid.* is used in both the second and third citations above, the three footnotes would of necessity be consecutive, although they could be on different pages of the thesis. Furthermore, it will be noted that use of this form permits reference to the same or to different pages of the work cited.

Although there is no technical limit to the number of pages that may intervene between two citations, the second of which consists of the form *ibid.*, common sense dictates that if many pages intervene it is better to repeat enough of the reference for it to be recognized, so that the reader will not have to search for the preceding footnote. It is never wrong to make a footnote complete without reference to any other footnote.

Op. cit.

● When references to the same work follow each other closely but not consecutively and when they are to different pages in that work, *op. cit.* (from the Latin *opere citado*, "the work cited") may be used in place of the title and facts of publication. The author's surname, generally without given name or initials, must be repeated (in order to identify the work cited), followed by the abbreviation *op. cit.* The page reference, or volume and page reference if necessary, closes the citation:

63Bernard Berenson, Rumor and Reflection (New York: Simon and Schuster, 1952), pp. 16-24.

64Fred M. Fling, Writing of History (New Haven: Yale University Press, 1930), pp. 52-84.

65Berenson, op. cit., p. 312. [Note that the references to Berenson are not consecutive and that different pages in his work are cited.]

66Fling, op. cit., pp. 29-31.

67Ibid. [This refers to Fling, pp. 29-31.]

Loc. cit.

● When a second but nonconsecutive reference is made to the exact material (i.e., the same volume and page) previously cited, *loc. cit.* (Latin *loco citato*, "the place cited") is substituted for *ibid.* or *op. cit.* The author's name, generally without given name or initials, must appear to identify the work. Page numbers *never* follow the form *loc. cit.*, for the simple reason that they are unnecessary.

68Sisley Huddleston, Europe in Zigzags (Philadelphia: J. B. Lippincott Company, 1929), p. 350.

69William S. Sonnenschein, The Best Books (New York: G. P. Putnam's Sons, 1923), pp. 42-52.

70Huddleston, loc. cit. [This abbreviation is used because the reference is to page 350. Citation of any other page or pages would have called for the use of op. cit., followed by a page number.]

A brief recapitulation may help the thesis writer: (1) *Ibid.* is used in consecutive footnotes that refer to the same work, whether to the same or different pages. (2) *Op. cit.* is used with nonconsecutive footnotes that refer to the same work but to different pages. (3) *Loc. cit.* is used with nonconsecutive footnotes that refer to the same work and to the same page, or pages, of that work. It is better, if several thesis pages intervene between two footnote references to the same work, to repeat enough of the material previously given to obviate the necessity for the reader to look back, perhaps with some waste of time, to find the preceding citation.

When references are made to two or more books or articles by the same author, the forms *op. cit.* and *loc. cit.* are not used in subsequent citations, and enough of the facts concerning the author and the titles of the works must in each case be given to distinguish each one beyond the possibility of confusion to the reader.

Other forms of abbreviation

● In referring to passages within the student's own thesis or to another source, certain abbreviated expressions are used in footnote reference. Cf. (*confer*, "compare") is used to suggest comparison with another passage or statement. Cf. *ante* (*confer ante*, "compare above") is used, with page number as a cross-reference to direct comparative attention to preceding material in the thesis; similarly, cf. *post* (*confer post*, "compare below"), with the page reference, points to a comparison with subsequent matter. *Supra* ("above") is used for a cross-reference to any preceding matter, while *infra* ("below") is used for cross-reference to any subsequent matter in the manuscript. It will be noted that the last two forms are mere references to content and do not call for *comparison* of the trains of thought.

As far as is possible, definite page citations should be given. However, the use of such forms as "pp. 5 f." or "pp. 5 *et seq.*" (page 5 and the following page) and "pp. 5 ff." or "pp. 5 *et seqq.*" (page 5 and the following pages) is permissible when the data referred to extend brokenly over several pages. These forms are used to indicate that the matter referred to is found on pages beginning with the one cited and continuing rather indefinitely, while *et passim* ("and here and there") is used to indicate that the matter referred to is not found within definite page limits in the work cited but is scattered about. These vague or blanket references are to be avoided whenever possible.

Glossary

● In parenthetical literary references, in the footnotes, and in bibliographical material, many abbreviations have been adopted to save time for both reader and writer. The following, many of which are discussed in detail in the preceding paragraphs or elsewhere in this book, are standard:

Art., Arts. — article, articles	Art. iii; Arts. iv and vi
Bk., Bks. — book, books	Bk. I; Bks. III–V
c., or *ca.* (*circa*) — about	*ca.* 1473 (used to indicate an approximate date)
cf. (*confer*) — compare	
cf. *ante* (*confer ante*) — compare above	
cf. *post* (*confer post*) — compare below	
Chap., Chaps. — chapter, chapters	Chap. II; Chaps. III–VI
Col., Cols. — column, columns	Col. 6; Cols. 9–11
Div., Divs. — division, divisions	Div. III; Divs. IV and V
ed., eds. — editor (or edited), editors	
ed., edd. — edition, editions	
e.g. (*exempli gratia*) — for example	
et al. (*et alii*) — and others	
et seq., *et seqq.* (*et sequens*) — and the following	(See below under "pp.")
et passim — and here and there	
f., ff. — and the following	(See below under "pp.")

Fig., Figs. — figure, figures	Fig. 7; Figs. 8 and 9
ibid. (*ibidem*) — the same reference	
idem — the same person	
i.e. (*id est*) — that is	
illus. — illustrator, illustrated	
infra — below	
l., ll. — line, lines	l. 8; ll. 10–12
loc. cit. (*loco citato*) — the place cited	
n., nn. — note, notes (footnotes)	n. 9; nn. 6 and 7
n.d. — no date	
n.n. — no name	
n.p. — no place	
No., Nos. — number, numbers	No. 1; Nos. 2–6
op. cit. (*opere citato*) — in the work cited	
p., pp. — page, pages	p. 5; pp. 5–7 (signifies pages 5 to 7 inclusive)
pp. 4 f., or pp. 4 *et seq.* — page 4 and the following page	
pp. 5 ff., or pp. 5 *et seqq.* — page 5 and the following pages	
par., pars. — paragraph, paragraphs	par. 6; pars. 7 and 12
passim — here and there	
Pt., Pts. — part, parts	Pt. I; Pts. II and III
q. v. (*quod vide*) — which see	
rev. — revised, revision	rev. ed. — revised edition
Sec., Secs. — section, sections	Sec. 4; Secs. 6–9
sic — thus	
supra — above	
trans. — translator, translated	
vide — see	
Vol., Vols. — volume, volumes	Vol. I; Vols. II–X

V. GENERAL RULES REGARDING CITATIONS

Secondary source citations

• The footnote citation indicates the exact source to which the writer is indebted, whether it is primary or secondary. The writer's authority is always the work consulted. Standards of scholarly work demand the use of first-hand sources; but where this is not possible and the writer must quote another writer, the risk of error should cause him to take the precaution of indicating the secondary nature of his reference. A source known only through a secondary work must be so indicated by the form used in the citation.

[71]Archer B. Hulbert, Portage Paths (Cleveland: Arthur H. Clark, 1903), p. 181, citing Jesuit Relations and Allied Documents, Vol. LIX, p. 41.

The reverse order of this citation follows:

[72]Jesuit Relations and Allied Documents, Vol. LIX, p. 41, cited by Archer B. Hulbert, Portage Paths (Cleveland: Arthur H. Clark, 1903), p. 181.

This also would indicate that the writer had not examined the original material but had relied on Hulbert's citation. The order of these forms is not to be regarded as interchangeable; the precedence of authorities should be determined by the emphasis required in the particular case. For example, if the fact that Hulbert cites the material is the important consideration, the first order should be employed; if the material itself is of primary significance, the second form may be used.

Series of citations from the same source

● If several facts, or alleged facts, drawn from the same source are presented consecutively, it is permissible to cite the source but once, at the conclusion of the paragraph or even of a series of paragraphs, if the continuity of the passage is clear to the eye. If there is any possibility of doubt or confusion on the part of the reader, the citation should be given at the end of each paragraph. It is advisable to indicate, in the initial note, the fact that the paragraphs are from a single source.

Points of style

● In the case of writers of wide reputation, it is customary to omit the given name and/or initials, in accordance with the permissible practice of so-called "academic familiarity." Exception is made in instances when confusion of identity might be possible, as, for example, John Stuart Mill and James Mill, both eminent in the same field, or when a prominent person is commonly known by a compound name or title, such as Babe Ruth or Madame Schumann-Heink.

Abbreviation of titles of address

● Titles such as Doctor and Professor are omitted in references. Inclusion of a title, however, is permissible to insure clarity in identifying or placing a person in relation to a particular field. For example, inclusion of the title "Professor" Koos or "President" Calles in a reference in a thesis in the English Department identifies an individual who is not peculiarly associated with the special field of English.

Shortened titles, such as Prof., Gen., Capt., and the like, are considered poor form, although abbreviations are acceptable in the following cases: Mr., Messrs., Mrs., and their foreign equivalents; Dr., St., Rev., and Hon., preceding personal names; and Esq., Sr., and Jr., following personal names.

Rules for capitalization of titles

● In titles of books, journals, and magazine articles, the common practice is to capitalize all the principal words: nouns, pronouns, adjectives, adverbs, verbs, and first and last words. Special rules governing the capitalization of titles in the commoner foreign languages may be found in *A Manual of Style* of the University of Chicago Press.

Rule for underscoring titles

● The major title — the title of a book, a journal, or a periodical — is underscored. This should be underscored whether it appears in the text, in a footnote, or in the bibliography. The titles of essays, plays, and the like, which have a book format, and of pamphlets, documentary references, newspapers, and journals, should be underscored to indicate the use of italics.

When a title is cited that occurs *within* a book, in a periodical, or as a chapter of a text, it is not underscored but is enclosed in quotation marks. Only titles of publications having book format are underscored.

Although it is permissible to italicize a word, or words, in the text or footnotes for the purpose of emphasis, this practice should be distinctly exceptional, or the emphasis will be diminished and the intended effect lessened or lost.

Foreign words or phrases are underscored except in the following instances: (1) when they have become Anglicized; (2) when they occur frequently in a technical sense in a given discussion; or (3) when the foreign matter quoted is extensive. Manuals of style usually contain lists of words which, in the opinion of their authors, are to be considered Anglicized. Special usages for foreign languages, for certain scientific materials, and for legal and historical forms may also be found in these manuals.

A student whose thesis contains much material in a foreign language should consult his adviser about the most acceptable system for underscoring in his particular situation. General rules regarding this matter are found to have exceptions in some institutions.

Use of numerals in footnote references

● Roman capitals (III, IV) are used for the volume, book, part, or division of a book which has book format, and for the volume number of a periodical.

Small Roman numerals (ii, xxix) are used for those pages so numbered within a book, for example, the preface, and for scenes of a play.

Arabic numerals are used to designate the individual issues of periodicals and the text pages of a book or a magazine article.

To connect the numbers indicating consecutive pages, the hundreds may be omitted from the second number, thus using only two figures, except when the first number ends in two ciphers, necessitating repetition of the whole form. It is not necessary to repeat a cipher in the second number if the next to the last figure is a cipher. Illustrations: 47–48; 55–69; 241–48; 300–307; 106–7; 1813–16.

Names of books of the Bible, both canonical and apocryphal, the titles of ancient manuscripts, and all symbols used to designate manuscripts should have initial letters capitalized, and references to divisions thereof should be indicated with Arabic numerals; thus, Psalms 53:10.

In references to passages from plays, the clearest printed form possible gives acts in capital Roman numerals, scenes in lower-case Roman numerals, and lines in Arabic numerals, the three divisions being separated by commas; thus, *Hamlet* III, ii, 28–196. Some authors, however, prefer to indicate the acts by small Roman numerals, scenes by Arabic numerals, and lines by Arabic numerals, the three divisions being separated by periods; thus, *Hamlet* iii. 2. 28–196. Whichever form is employed should be adhered to consistently throughout the thesis.

5 | TABLES AND ILLUSTRATIONS

SINCE A TABLE OR AN ILLUSTRATION is used to convey ideas to the reader, due care should be exercised in the selection of material to be contained therein. Needless repetition or childish simplicity in presenting facts is to be deprecated. A thesis is a report of a scholarly nature and is to be read by people who will readily understand well-presented ideas. When a straightforward statement will suffice, illustrative materials need not be used.

Because of the varied nature of its contents, this chapter is divided into two parts: the first giving information related to tables, and the second, information related to other kinds of illustrations.

I. TABLES

The data collected for a thesis must be presented as evidence upon which conclusions are based. If the data are of a statistical nature, they are usually organized in the form of tables or graphs, or both. In fact, when many numbers are presented to the reader, for the sake of brevity they should be tabulated or charted. Long strings of numbers in the body of the thesis will inevitably defeat any effort to produce smooth writing, and the reader may, because of them, lose the deeper meanings to be drawn from the results reported. The reader is usually more interested in conclusions than in minute details. Thus, although complete data should be provided at some place in the thesis, for the benefit of those who want full details, the text should contain the findings, or conclusions, stated in comprehensive terms, and it should not be clogged with masses of statistical minutiae.

Not all statistical matter need be in tabular form; if it may smoothly be woven into the context, so much the better; for example, the ensuing facts should not be tabulated if they stand alone: "The 607 delegates, representing seventeen nations, voted 402 to 205 in favor of the resolution." A very simple array of facts may be presented in tabular form that is still not a formally organized table and is not, therefore, included in the list of tables:

and the class members were about evenly divided on the candidates, as is shown in these results:

	Boys	Girls	Totals
For Smith	17	16	33
For Brown	13	15	28
Total	30	31	61

A table should possess unity, that is to say, only one general kind or type of data should be presented in one table. Normally, an analytical table sets forth several related variables to make comprehensible a series of facts. A table should be as simple as the material and purposes will permit it to be. This does not imply that a table may not have several columns of data, but it does mean that one table should not try to convey too many ideas and relationships. The ingenuity of the reader should not be taxed in an effort to interpret what is presented; the table is supposed to help the reader, not test his intelligence. Lastly, a table, especially one in the body of the thesis, should be brief. Very long tables normally belong in the appendix, or they may be filed in a library and a reference to them given at the appropriate point, or points, in the thesis.

Placement of tables

• Since a table contains material that will be discussed in the text, or that is essential to a clear understanding or interpretation of what has been written, it should appear as near as possible to the discussion that relates to it. If the table has fewer than four or five enumerated items per column, it may be placed on the page with the discussion of its contents. In general, however, each table is placed on a separate page, and no portion of context is typed on that page. The reason for this rule is that it is much easier for the typist to reproduce the materials when it is agreed that each table is to occupy a separate page; the problems of accurate reference to the table, correct spacing, width of margins, and possible use of another size of type, such as Elite rather than Pica, are simply eliminated by this practice.

Under no circumstances should a table precede the first discussion of its contents. If the table is short and is to be placed on a page with context but cannot be accommodated on the page where first mention of it occurs, it should normally be placed on the next page at the end of the first paragraph. In typewritten manuscript, a short table does not look well at the very top of a page of context.

Relating tables to context

• The reader will more readily understand a table if he is given a brief introduction to it. This may consist of an explanation of the manner of presenting the data or a discussion of their general import, or both. It is essential to set forth at some point the significant conclusions made possible by the data presented. Two rules hold with regard to the relationship between tables and context: (1) A table must be so constructed that it may be read and understood without reference to the text of the thesis (some readers look at tables only and do not read the text); and (2) the text of the thesis should be so complete that the major train of thought may be followed without perusal of any of the tables. If a table is not too complex, if its organization is well thought out, and if all captions are complete, those who want to grasp only what is contained in the tables will have little difficulty. But since the typical reader does not like to read tables and will do so only as a matter of necessity, the thesis writer will be well advised to incorporate into the body of his thesis enough generalizations derived from the tables to make for easy reading and for a generalized, though not a specific and detailed, understanding of them.

If a table occurs on the page with, or immediately following, the first discussion of its contents, only the number of the table (not the page number) need be given. If, however, reference is made to a table at any point other than on the same or the preceding page, *both* the table number and number of the page on which it occurs must be given, to help the reader.

Because it is easy to interpret erroneously the phrases "in the following table" and "in the above table," reference should usually be by table number, or by both table and page numbers. It is as easy to say, "Table III shows . . . ," as to say, "The following table shows . . ." Moreover, it is clearer and more accurate.

These practices are illustrated on page 90.

Numbering tables

● Tables should be numbered consecutively throughout the thesis, from first to last, even if some of them appear in the appendix. The practice is to use capital Roman numerals in numbering tables. The word TABLE, in full caps, followed by the appropriate number, is placed one double space above the caption, and centered on it.

Table captions

● Each table in a thesis must have a caption, or title, that tells concisely just what it contains. The caption should be placed *above* a table but *below* an illustration.

The numbers and captions of tables must correspond exactly to the numbers and captions enumerated in the list of tables in the introductory section of the thesis.

Table captions should be written in full capital letters. Although the usual rules regarding punctuation and abbreviation hold within the caption, no period is placed at the end.

The caption should be centered with respect to the material on the page. If it runs to two or more lines, it should be arranged in the form of an inverted pyramid, that is, with the first line the longest.

When a table will fit on a page broadside but not in normal position, it is so placed that the caption will be on the binding side, easily read when the table is rotated one-quarter turn clockwise.

Superfluous words, such as "table showing" or "chart representing," should be avoided in all captions; the mere fact that the material has been arranged for tabular or graphic illustration implies that something is "shown" or "represented."

Column captions

● Each column in a table should have an appropriate descriptive caption so placed that the possibility of confusion will be reduced to a minimum and so arranged that it will form a neat body of typed material. The normal rules governing punctuation, capitalization, and abbreviation should be followed in preparing these headings, with terminal punctuation generally omitted.

Each column heading should be centered between the vertical ruled lines that enclose it, or in the space allotted to its column if there are no vertical rulings. When a heading is so long that placing it in normal reading position is not feasible, it may be run diagonally upward and to the right from the column, or vertically from the column. (See table on pages 94 and 95.)

Numbered columns

● When a table is made up of numerous columns, and frequent reference to specific columns is to be made, the student will find it convenient to number them, starting with the stub (the first column in a table) and numbering *all* columns from left to right. Each such number should be enclosed in parentheses, (1), (2), (3), etc. Employment of this device makes for easy and accurate reference to the exact material intended.

Alignment and spacing of items in columns

● Columns that consist of words are aligned on the left, as is a margin. Columns of numbers are aligned on the right, except that when there are decimal points in a column it is these that must be aligned. The following will illustrate the correct procedure:

```
Number of samples included . . . . . . . . 324
Number of titrations made . . . . . . . .   6
Average of findings . . . . . . . . . . .  32.6
Mean variation of findings . . . . . . .    2.456
```

In columns with vertical rulings, there should be at least one blank space on each side of the largest number in the column. When vertical rulings are not inserted, the columns must be separated by enough space so that each will stand out as a separate item and will be easy for the reader to follow without a mechanical guide.

The horizontal lines of material in a table are usually single-spaced, although when a break is indicated, when the number of items is small, or when single-spacing will make the table look unbalanced, the lines may be double-spaced. The criteria are neatness of appearance and ease of reading, not absolute rules.

Omission of zero, degree and dollar signs, and other items

• In a column of numbers, the zero in front of a decimal may be omitted from all except the first and the last lines. When figures dealing with money are presented in a column of a table, the dollar sign should be used only before the first figure in the column and before the total. However, if not all figures in the column are in the same unit, the dollar sign should precede each entry where it is needed. Items not bearing the dollar sign will thus be known to be in other than monetary units. The same rules hold for columns in which the sign for degrees (of heat, or arc of a circle) is used.

When an item must be omitted from its normal place in a table, the omission should be indicated by a blank space, by dashes (- - -), or by dots (. . .). The blank space is usually preferable. A zero (0) should not be used for this purpose unless the value that is supposed to appear at that point is actually zero. If the author wishes to show why the item is missing, he may insert a superscript, in parentheses, and in a footnote at the bottom of the table give the necessary explanation.

Table footnotes

• When it is necessary further to elaborate a point within the body of a table or in the caption, a footnote should be used. The rules for insertion of such a footnote are given on page 22.

Ruling tables

• No absolute regulations are possible for the use of solid lines in the construction of tables, except that the author must be consistent. Rules are used in tables to guide the eyes of the reader and to prevent errors. Thus, if they may be omitted without increasing the possibility of error and misreading, they should be left out.

Double horizontal rules should be placed at the top of the table, a single horizontal rule below the column headings, and single or double horizontal rules at the bottom of the table.

Vertical rules should be used in tables of several columns or when the columns are so arranged or are so close together that the reader may be confused. Three methods are commonly used to make the vertical rules: (1) While the table is being typed, a vertical line of apostrophes or of colons will serve as a guide, although the finished product does not have an entirely professional look. This method is fast, all copies are exactly alike, and everything on each copy is exactly the same color. (2) The vertical rules may be made by inserting the page in the typewriter on its side, after the numbers have been typed, and using the underscore key. Only one copy can be ruled at a time without risk of error. (3) The vertical rules may be made with black India ink and a straightedge. Although the typewriter ribbon and the ink are not identical in color, the lines do not overlap, each can be accurately placed, and the width may be varied if desired. When a table is doubled (two equal parts are placed side by side), a double vertical rule is used to separate the two halves.

It is permissible to leave some extra space below each line, or group of lines, for ease in reading the table. If this is done, however, care must be exercised not to confuse the reader by the blank spaces, whether they occur at regular or irregular intervals.

Horizontal rules between lines of items are not commonly used in typed tables. If, however, the material is so spaced that confusion might result, these lines may be inserted to guide the reader, as shown in the table on page 93. In other instances, guide dots may be run out to the first column of figures, or the space intervening at the right between the end of the wording and the columns may be left blank. Samples of all these variations are shown on pages 89 to 93.

Whatever style he chooses, the student must remember that once he has established a set of rules for his own guidance, he must then be consistent.

Continued tables

● When a table is so long that it must be continued on the next page, or ensuing pages, the entire arrangement on each such page is the same as on the first, except that only the table number and the parenthesized word "continued" replace the table number and the original caption.

First page of the table:

TABLE XV

ANALYSIS OF RESULTS OBTAINED BY USING
A SILVER NITRATE SOLUTION

On the second and following pages:

TABLE XV (continued)

Very large tables

● When a table is merely long but not excessively wide, it may be typed on regular $8\frac{1}{2}'' \times 11''$ paper and continued on several consecutive pages, following the plan described in the paragraph above. When, however, the table is too wide to fit on the regular size of paper, even when turned broadside, one of two plans may be followed: (1) the table may be typed on very large paper and folded into the thesis, or (2) the table may be photostatically reduced to the size of the thesis page. Because the latter method saves time and bulk, it is preferable, if the reduction is not so drastic as to make necessary the use of a magnifying glass to read the table.

If the system of folding is decided upon, the table should be so folded as not to exceed eight inches at its widest point. This will permit the table to be bound into the thesis in such a way that the trimming knives used in binding will not cut it in two. It is usually not permissible to fold a table from the bottom or the top; but if this is absolutely necessary, the table should be folded up from the bottom so as to be not over ten and one-half inches in length, and placed with its top flush with the top edges of the other pages of the thesis. This, again, will prevent the table from being cut when the thesis is trimmed in the binding process.

Table margins

● Whether or not the page of typed material contains a table, it is desirable to keep a margin of one and one-half inches on the left-hand (or binder) side and margins of at least one inch on the three other sides. But by turning the table broadside, or in some cases by slightly exceeding these margins, the typist will be able to get even a large table on a page of regular paper. In situations of this kind, the left-hand margin must never be less than one inch or the other margins less than one-half inch, because of binding and trimming requirements.

Pagination of tables

● Each page containing a table must have a page number. This is placed in its normal position, even if the table is placed broadside on the page. If the usual margins are exceeded, in an effort to fit the table onto the paper, the number will have to be slightly displaced toward the upper right-hand corner of the page, but it should appear in approximately its stipulated place.

Accuracy

● There must be absolute accuracy in presenting data in tables. If the student wants to round off his numbers, he may do so provided that he clearly indicates to the reader the extent to which the numbers have been rounded off.

Each item in a table should be checked in the final copy, since errors frequently creep in during repeated copying of the figures. This point cannot be stressed too emphatically; accuracy is essential, even at the cost of repeated checking.

II. ILLUSTRATIONS

The term "Figure" (always capitalized to avoid confusion with the uncapitalized word meaning a number) is used to denote any kind of graphic illustration other than a table. A Figure may be a chart, diagram, drawing, graph, photograph, photostat, map, histogram, blueprint, or any other type of illustration.

Facts are readily grasped when properly presented in visual form, and good illustrations are therefore more popular today than ever before. The average reader derives more benefit from an illustration than from a table or a word description of the data. Because the public is so accustomed to graphic presentations of superior quality, crude or shoddy work will be severely criticized or ridiculed. The student who plans to use illustrations must know that he possesses, or has ready access to, the skill and processes required for a satisfactory finished product.

Because illustrations are so helpful in presenting information, a word of caution should be sounded: As a general rule, Figures are not both easily and inexpensively reproduced. The student should carefully investigate the problems of duplication (getting his information from those who will do the work) and the matter of cost before building his thesis around numerous complex illustrations.

An illustration should present only one fact or a series of related facts, and it should be easy to interpret. Any method of depicting ideas that is not clear and easily comprehended will not be understood by the average reader. Stress is given to this point by the Standards for Graphic Presentation, quoted on page 53, and the Check List for Illustrations, page 54. Useful guides for preparing Figures of all kinds will be found in books devoted to graphic presentation, some of which are listed in the Bibliography, pages 68–69.

Hand-drawn illustrations

• Because hand-drawn illustrations are so frequently used in reporting research, the three commonest forms are discussed here. They are: line or curve charts; bar graphs or charts; and area or volume graphs, such as pie, rectangle, or concentric-circle charts.

1. *Line or curve charts* are plotted on rectangular co-ordinate paper and are so well known and so widely used that even school children are taught to read them. The relationship between two variables is depicted. The data have a range of some kind, such as time, age, distance, or weight. By placing two or more lines on the same chart, comparison between the several series may often be presented to the reader. Figure 3, page 96, illustrates several of the principles of preparing a chart of this kind.

2. *Bar graphs or charts* consist of a series of bars or lines arranged to show the relationship, or relationships, among certain data or groups of data. These may be divided into two general classes: (1) those with bars of different lengths, for direct comparison of lengths (each bar, or line, may in turn be shaded to show varying degrees of component parts), and (2) charts with all bars of the same length, usually representing 100 per cent, or some other unit, with shaded subdivisions to allow comparison of the component elements. Examples of both types may be seen in Figures 5 and 6 in the Appendix, pages 97 and 99.

3. *Area or volume charts* show relationships between, or among, quantities, each of which is represented by an area or volume. The so-called pie chart is the best known of this category. A common method of emphasizing some one element in the total consists in arranging the pie to look as though a slice (the factor to be stressed) has been cut and slightly withdrawn. The two pies in Figure 8, page 101, illustrate these points.

Placement of Figures

• Since a Figure contains ideas that will be discussed in the text or that are essential to a clear understanding of what has been written, it should be placed as near as possible to the discussion that relates to it. This allows for three possibilities:

(1) the Figure may be placed on the very next page, with no context typed on that page; (2) it may appear at a lower point on the same page with the first reference to it; or (3) if the first reference occurs near the bottom of the page, it may be placed on the following page, usually at the end of the first paragraph. In typewritten manuscript, an illustration does not look well when placed at the very top of a page with text below it. Under no circumstances should a Figure appear in the manuscript before the first discussion of its content.

As a general rule, because of the art work and special paper required, each Figure is placed on a separate page. This does not eliminate the possibility of having several Figures on the same page, if this arrangement works out normally with the development of the thesis; nor does it mean that, when regular typing paper is used, context cannot be typed on the unused portions of the page on which a Figure is drawn. The sole reason for placing each Figure on a separate page that carries no typed material is to eliminate the possibility of having to repeat the art work if any retyping is necessary.

Relating illustrations to context

● The reader will more readily understand the concepts contained in a Figure if he is given a brief introduction to it. This may consist of an explanation of the manner of presenting the data or a discussion of their general import, or both. In any case, the significant conclusions that derive from the presentation must be set forth at some point. It is the responsibility of the writer, not the reader, to make a critical analysis of the data presented.

Two rules hold with regard to the relationship between illustrations and context: (1) an illustration must be so designed that it may be read and understood without reference to the text of the thesis (some readers look at illustrations only and do not read the text); and (2) the text of the thesis should be so complete that the major train of thought may be followed without careful examination of the illustrations. If the Figure is not too complex, if its organization is well thought out, and if all captions are complete, those who want to grasp only what is shown in it will have no difficulty. The text should, however, contain enough exposition to give a generalized, although not a specific and detailed, understanding of the illustrative materials.

If a Figure occurs on the page with, or immediately following, the first discussion of its contents, only the number of the Figure (and not the page on which it is located) need be given. If, however, reference is made to an illustration at any point other than on the same or the preceding page, *both* the Figure and page numbers must be given. If one is to err in this connection, it is better to give the reader too much rather than too little information to help him find the illustration.

Because it is easy to misinterpret the phrases "in the following Figure" and "in the above illustration," reference is preferably by Figure number, or by both Figure and page numbers. It is as easy to say, "Figure IV shows . . ." as to say, "The following illustration shows . . . ," and it is more accurate.

Numbering Figures

● Most frequently, the total number of all of the various kinds of illustrations is small. In this case all are grouped together as one series and are called Figures. When, however, there are several of any one kind, it is proper to call this group by its specific name and to call the others Figures. For example, a thesis may contain an entire series of maps, numbered separately from other illustrations, and in addition a series of Figures, including all illustrative material other than tables and maps.

Arabic numerals are used in numbering Figures. If there are two or more series — for example, maps and Figures — each series starts with an Arabic 1. The number should be *below* the illustration, one double space above the caption.

Captions for Figures

● Each Figure must have a caption, or a title, that tells concisely just what it presents. The caption should appear *below* the illustration, one double space below the Figure number. The numbers and captions in the list of Figures should correspond exactly to those given in the table of contents.

The caption may be typed or lettered (draughtsmen's letters in black India ink) in full capital letters blocked in inverted-pyramid form (longest line on top) and without terminal punctuation, or in caps and lower-case letters in paragraph or underhung form with terminal punctuation. In any case, the usual rules for punctuation and abbreviation are followed within the caption. The following examples are of the same caption presented in the three different ways:

FIGURE 8

COMPARATIVE RESULTS OBTAINED FROM ANALYSES
OF WATER SAMPLES GATHERED IN ELEVEN
DISTRIBUTED GEOGRAPHICAL AREAS

Figure 8. Comparative results obtained from analyses of water samples gathered in eleven distributed geographical areas.

Figure 8. Comparative results obtained from analysis of water samples gathered in eleven distributed geographical areas.

Superfluous phrases, such as "graph showing" or "chart representing," should be avoided. The fact that material is being shown or represented in graphic or other illustrative form is self-evident.

Footnotes to Figures
● When the writer wants to elaborate or explain some item in a Figure, a footnote should be used. The rules for insertion of such a footnote will be found in Chapter 4, page 22.

Paper for illustrations
● Because of the many possible kinds of illustrations and the many kinds of paper available for everything from line graphs to color photography, no attempt will be made to go into this matter here. Two general suggestions, however, may prove helpful. (1) One should discuss with an expert, such as an employee of the duplicating division of the university, a member of the architecture department, or a representative of a commercial firm, the appropriate paper for the kind of illustration planned. (2) If the thesis is to be microfilmed — and more and more institutions are microfilming all theses and dissertations — one should investigate the advantages and limitations of various kinds of paper in relation to this process. For example, co-ordinate paper with very light blue lines is generally required. For some processes, only black India ink (no other color) photographs well. The speed with which new and simpler processes are being developed makes it impossible to give instructions that will remain up to date for even a year at a time. The important thing is for the student to be aware of the special problems posed by illustrations, and prepared to seek technical advice if necessary — particularly if he plans to use many illustrations in a thesis that is to be microfilmed.

Very large illustrations
● When a Figure is too large to fit on a page of the standard 8½″ × 11″ size, it may be folded into the thesis, or it may be photostatically reduced to the proper size. Because the latter method saves time and bulk, it is preferable, if the reduction is not so drastic as to make the use of a magnifying glass necessary.

If the system of folding is decided upon, the Figure should be so folded as not to exceed eight inches at its widest point. This will permit the Figure to be bound into the thesis in such a way that the trimming knives used in binding will not cut it in two. It is usually not permissible to fold a Figure from the bottom or the top; but if this is absolutely necessary, the page should be folded up from the bottom so as not to exceed ten and one-half inches in length, and placed with its upper edge flush with the top edges of the other pages of the thesis. This, again, will prevent it from being cut when the thesis is trimmed in the binding process.

Mounting illustrations

● A photograph, map, printed form, or other illustration smaller than regular page size should be mounted on thesis paper with stationer's rubber cement, following exactly the directions on the container. The entire area of both surfaces to be joined must be coated and allowed to dry for a while before they are placed together. Excess cement may readily be wiped off with a dry cloth. Wrinkling of the paper is eliminated by using rubber cement rather than a water paste. Also, discoloration of this and other pages of the thesis can be avoided by allowing the cemented materials to dry thoroughly before being placed against other pages of the finished thesis. It is generally possible to plan the mounting of small illustrations in such a way that the captions may be typed in at the proper points.

Pagination of Figures

● Each page containing a Figure should have a page number placed in the normal position. A folded page, irrespective of its size, carries only one page number, and the sheet should be so folded that this number will appear in its regular place.

Standards for graphic presentation

● The following list of rules or standards for graphic presentation was prepared by a joint committee of the American Society of Mechanical Engineers.

1. The general arrangement of a diagram should proceed from left to right.

2. Where possible, represent quantities by linear magnitude, as areas or volumes are more likely to be misinterpreted.

3. For a curve, the vertical scale, whenever practicable, should be so selected that the zero line will appear in the diagram.

4. If the zero line of the vertical scale will not normally appear in the curve diagram, the zero line should be shown by the use of a horizontal break in the diagram.

5. The zero lines of the scales for a curve should be sharply distinguished from the other co-ordinate lines.

6. For curves having a scale representing percentages, it is usually desirable to emphasize in some distinctive way the 100 per cent line used as a basis of comparison.

7. When the scale of the diagram refers to dates, and the period represented is not a complete unit, it is better not to emphasize the first and last ordinates, since such a diagram does not represent the beginning and end of time.

8. When curves are drawn on logarithmic co-ordinates, the limiting lines of the diagram should each be of some power of 1— on the logarithmic scale.

9. It is advisable not to show any more co-ordinate lines than are necessary to guide the eye in reading the diagram.

10. The curve lines of a diagram should be sharply distinguished from the ruling.

11. In curves representing a series of observations, it is advisable, whenever possible, to indicate clearly on the diagram all the points representing the separate observations.

12. The horizontal scale for curves should usually read from left to right and the vertical scale from bottom to top.

13. Figures for the scale of a diagram should be placed at the left and at the bottom or along the respective axes.

14. It is often desirable to include in the diagram the numerical data or formulae represented.

15. If numerical data are not included in the diagram, it is desirable to give the data in tabular form accompanying the diagram.

16. All lettering and all figures in a diagram should be placed so as to be easily read from the base as the bottom or from the right-hand edge of the diagram as the bottom.

17. The title of a diagram should be made as clear and complete as possible. Subtitles or descriptions should be added if necessary to insure clearness.[1]

---

[1] *Report of the Joint Committee of the American Society of Mechanical Engineers on Standards for Graphic Presentation.* Copies of this report may be secured from the American Society of Mechanical Engineers, 29 West 39th Street, New York City.

Check list for illustrations

● The student may find it helpful, when his illustrations are ready for final art work, to check each one against the following list:

1. Are the data correct?
2. Has the best method been used for showing the data?
3. Are the proportions of the illustration the best possible to show the data?
4. Are all scales in place?
5. Have the scales been selected and placed in the best possible manner?
6. Are the points accurately plotted?
7. Are the numerical figures for the data shown?
8. Have the figures for the data been copied correctly?
9. Can the figures for the data be added and the total shown?
10. Are all dates accurately shown?
11. Is the zero of the vertical scale shown?
12. Are all zero lines and the 100-per-cent lines made broad enough?
13. Is all the lettering placed in the proper directions for reading?
14. Is cross-hatching well made, with lines evenly spaced?
15. Are dimension lines used wherever advantageous?
16. Is a key or legend necessary?
17. Does the key or legend correspond to the drawing?
18. Is there a complete, clear, and concise title?
19. Is the drafting work of good quality?
20. Have all pencil lines which might show been erased?
21. Is the illustration in every way ready to mark O.K.? [2]

---

[2] Adapted from William C. Brinton, *Graphic Methods for Presenting Facts* (New York: The Engineering Magazine Company, 1914), pp. 361–63. Permission to use granted by McGraw-Hill Book Company.

6 | TYPING AIDS

MANY STUDENTS TYPE their own theses, at least in the initial stages; others have them typed by workers who are not familiar with thesis form and university requirements. For both of these groups and for others as well, the following pages supply details that will aid in producing a more satisfactory finished typescript than otherwise would be possible. The suggestions are not given in an attempt to bring about a higher degree of standardization than now exists, desirable as that may be; their chief purpose is to make the task of preparing a typed manuscript easier than is now the case and to eliminate waste of time and materials.

Typing final copy

● Unless the thesis writer is a proficient typist, an expert should be employed to type the final copy of the thesis. A university official can usually supply the name of a capable typist. An expert will charge somewhat more per page than a less-experienced person, but in the long run his work may be cheaper than that of the amateur. If only a few pages of the latter's work have to be discarded, the cost of the wasted time and paper will more than offset the small extra sum charged by the competent typist. Moreover, the satisfaction attendant upon the production of a superior product is so great that the student should not forego this pleasure for a few dollars.

Typewriter

● A typewriter with large type (Pica, which has ten spaces to the inch) is most commonly required for all parts of the thesis except tables so large that smaller characters must be used. The sample pages in the back of this manual are set in Pica typewriter type, with only one exception — the large table on pages 94 and 95. If the student plans to present the final copy of his thesis in small type (Elite, with twelve spaces to the inch), he should submit a sample to the proper authority and secure approval before the final typing is undertaken.

With the development of electric typewriters, more and more institutions are permitting theses to be prepared on them, because the work they do is generally superior to that of the older-style machines. Some of the new typewriters make it easy to produce a professional-looking page with "justified," or even, right-hand margin; and some of the type faces available make the typed material look like printed matter. As a precaution, the thesis writer should ascertain local regulations before preparing his work on one of these new typewriters.

In a small but ever-increasing number of cases, students have access to a Vari-typer, a machine that can produce typed matter with "justified" right-hand margins, prepare headings and captions in various styles and sizes of type, and generally lend the thesis the appearance of a printed book. Again, however, permission to submit the thesis typed in this way should be secured in advance.

Whatever machine is used, a plain type face is always in better taste for a thesis than italic, script, or some other unusual style.

A typewriter that has the acute accent mark ('), the plus symbol (+), the equals symbol (=), which combined with the plus provides the plus-and-minus symbol ($\pm$), and the square brackets ([]) will be found most useful in final manuscript work. Electric typewriters and the Vari-typer, some of which have more keys than a standard machine, often provide these characters. In case the needed symbols are not available, the student must letter them in by hand, with black India ink. The book, *Preparation of Scientific and Technical Papers*, by Trelease and Yule, listed in the Bibliography, page 69, will be helpful in this connection.

Clean type

• The type should be thoroughly cleaned before typing the final copy of the thesis. The use of a good cleaning gum or a liquid cleaner, at frequent intervals, will guarantee the best possible impression from the keys of the machine. Throughout the mechanical reproduction, the student will remember that his thesis is supposed to be a contribution to the field of knowledge and that nothing less than the highest standards of form, style, and finish are satisfactory.

Ribbon

• For typing the final copy of the thesis, a nearly-new black ribbon, light- or medium-inked rather than heavy-inked, should be put on the machine. The stroke required for several carbon copies will insure clear original-copy impressions from even the less-heavily-inked ribbon. Since the first few pages typed with a new ribbon are often unusually dark, a more nearly uniform color will be had if the ribbon is used a short while before work on the thesis is started.

For most makes of typewriters it is possible to get an attachment that permits use of carbon-paper ribbons. For best results, this kind of ribbon is used only once, thus guaranteeing an absolutely even and very satisfactory finished product.

Paper

• Most universities require the student to present two or three copies of his thesis or dissertation, typed on a good quality of bond paper, of sixteen- or twenty-pound weight, and eight and one-half inches by eleven inches in size.

Additional copies, for the student's own use or for presentation to his committee chairman, may be typed on lighter-weight paper. As a rule, when four copies are needed, the first two should be on the heavier paper (either sixteen- or twenty-pound) and the others on thirteen-pound stock; if five or more copies are wanted, the two first copies should be on the heavier paper and the remaining copies on eleven-pound stock.

It is desirable that all pages of any given copy of the thesis be identical in weight, color, and texture of paper. The one way to insure this is to buy an adequate supply of paper before starting to type the final copies.

Only one side of the paper may be used in the thesis work. No deviation from this rule is permitted.

Carbon

• A superior grade of medium-weight black carbon paper should be purchased for typing final copies of the thesis. A sufficient quantity for the whole job should be secured at one time, because it is frequently difficult, if the original supply is exhausted, to match the weight and color of that previously used.

Because such individual factors as size of type, hardness of platen, firmness of touch, and weight of paper affect the appearance of carbon copies, it is impossible to say with finality just how often the carbon should be changed in any given case, although it must be changed more frequently for third and later copies than for the second copy. Care must be taken to insure carbon copies that are clean, even in color, and sharp and clear as to letters. On the average, about six or seven pages may be typed before changing the carbon for the second copy, whereas for third, fourth, and later copies renewal after every four or five pages is about right.

Although the price of the finest bond and carbon may seem rather high, the writer should remember that the small difference in cost between cheap and superior materials may represent the difference between a shoddy and a superior typescript.

Special guide sheet

● There are numerous devices that indicate to the typist the point on the page where he is typing, and, hence, the correct place to begin the footnotes pertinent to the material on that page. The special guide sheet reproduced on page 73 is widely used. Copies may be obtained at The Book Store, University of Southern California, Los Angeles, or prepared by the typist. Heavy lines and numbers, red or red-and-black, on onion-skin or other thin paper provide a useful form. When this sheet is placed between the original copy and the first sheet of the carbon paper, the typist can read through to it and know exactly where he is working on the page.

If the margins are established on the typewriter so that they need not be seen on the special guide sheet, an even more readable device may be used. This consists in a sheet of paper, *nine* inches in width (rather than eight and one-half inches), with the lines of type numbered in both ascending and descending order from the point at which the first line of typed material appears on the page to the point at which all typing should end. These line numbers are placed on the extreme right-hand side of the sheet. When this is inserted between the original copy and the first sheet of carbon paper, the one-half inch with these numbers on it will stick out at the right beyond the other sheets. Thus the typist has it in sight all the time and always knows from it where he is vertically on the page. Since margins are not shown on this style, many workers prefer the model referred to in the above paragraph and shown on page 73, despite the lessened legibility that results from reading it through a sheet of bond paper.

Some typewriters come equipped with a device attached to the platen that can be set as the sheet is placed in the machine and will indicate exactly how many more lines may be typed before the page is filled. As time goes on, more and more manufacturers will develop some method of helping the typist keep oriented.

A clever method for attaching a numbered strip of paper to the platen (achieving the same result as the device described in the above paragraph) is detailed in the book by Cunningham and Patrick. (See the Bibliography, page 68.)

Whether a special guide sheet or other device is used, it must be remembered that twenty-five double-spaced lines, or their equivalent, are all that should be placed on any page of properly proportioned thesis work. If any deviation is necessary, not more than one single-spaced line above or below that limit is permissible. If, for example, a footnote at the bottom of the page runs beyond the limit of twenty-five double-spaced lines, it should not be allowed to go more than one single-spaced line beyond that point. If it ends before the twenty-fifth double-spaced line, the page should be so proportioned that it will not run short by more than one single-spaced line, unless it is the last page of a chapter or a section. The guide sheet helps the typist to end all pages at a more or less fixed point.

Inserting the page

● When the sheets of paper and carbon, together with the special guide sheet, have been properly stacked, they must be so inserted into the typewriter that all the top edges will be even. If the stacked paper is placed between the edges of a piece of folded paper, or the flap of an envelope, and run into the machine, the upper edges of all sheets will be aligned. The variable line-space device allows the upper edge of the paper to be brought exactly even with the line scale. The paper should then be elevated four double spaces and the page number placed so that the last digit falls on the right-hand margin of the page, one inch in from the edge of the paper. The first line of typed material is on the fifth double space from the upper edge of the paper. The special guide sheet has these points clearly marked.

Margins

● A left-hand margin of one and one-half inches, a right-hand margin of one inch, and top and bottom margins of about one and one-quarter inches, each, will make a page neat in appearance and adequate to normal binding demands. The six-inch line of typed matter (eight and one-half inches, minus the two margins) will hold sixty Pica-type, or seventy-two Elite-type, characters. The established point for beginning to type material on the page should be respected, even if, for lack of enough to fill it, the page runs short.

The rules for width of margins are relaxed somewhat in the case of a large illustration or a table that will fit comfortably on a page but not within the usual marginal limits. Even when this violation is permitted, enough room should be left for trimming and binding.

Although in typing manuscripts it is nearly impossible to make all lines equal in length, no line should extend beyond the right-hand margin. If a word cannot be included in its entirety or properly syllabified within this limit, the entire word should be placed on the next line. An effort should be made to eliminate as many divided words as possible, since a right-hand margin with a large number of hyphens does not look well. (See page 62 for instructions regarding division of words.)

How to center material on the page

● The material on any page of a thesis should be symmetrically arranged with reference to the center of the typed matter and not equidistant from the edges of the paper, because the left- and right-hand margins are not equal in width. Following the rules given above for margins, the center line would be four and one-half inches from the left-hand edge of the paper. This same point will be found by moving in thirty Pica-type spaces, or thirty-six Elite-type spaces, from the correct left-hand margin. The special guide sheet, page 73, has the center line printed on it.

The typist will find it handy to prepare, on a piece of heavy paper, a guide rule like that reproduced below, to aid in determining just where to start typing a centered caption, chapter number, chapter title, or table number, and the like:

```
Elite type
   30    25    20    15    10     5     0     5    10    15    20    25    30
```

```
Pica type
   25    20    15    10     5     0     5    10    15    20    25
```

Long captions should be divided into two or more lines, with the longest line at the top and each succeeding line shorter than the one preceding it. This arrangement is referred to as the inverted-pyramid style.

Unless a centered caption ends with a question mark or an exclamation point, it should have no terminal punctuation. Within the caption, the usual rules regarding punctuation, abbreviation, and capitalization are adhered to.

Line of indention

● A line of indention, which is constant for all indented material, is established seven spaces to the right of the left-hand margin. This distance is kept constant whether it is for a paragraph of the text, a paragraph of quoted material, or a footnote.

For long single-spaced quotations, a new margin is established four spaces in from the regular left-hand margin of the text; even in this case, however, no deviation from the line of paragraph indention is permitted. (See example on page 87.)

Alignment of Roman numerals

● When Roman numerals are arranged in an outline form, the right-hand column is aligned, as in the case of Arabic numerals. This will make the left-hand side uneven, but it is the accepted form. Due allowance must be made when starting a page to provide space for the larger numerals, for example, XXXIII. A column of these figures, as in a table of contents or list of tables, would appear as follows:

```
      I. . . . . . . . . . . . . . . . . . . . . . . .     1
     II. . . . . . . . . . . . . . . . . . . . . . . .     7
    III. . . . . . . . . . . . . . . . . . . . . . . .    18
    XIV. . . . . . . . . . . . . . . . . . . . . . . .    96
 XXXIII. . . . . . . . . . . . . . . . . . . . . . . .   109
```

Spacing between lines

• The major portion of the thesis will be double-spaced, but there are places where single spacing or triple spacing will be needed. Footnote and bibliography entries are single-spaced, with a double space between items. Lengthy quotations are indented, quotation marks are omitted, and the material single-spaced. A triple space (three single spaces) is allowed between the chapter number and its title, between the title of the chapter and the first line of the context, both before and after any centered caption, and between the last line of a paragraph and an underscored sidehead.

Unequal spaces between lines

• There are some places in the thesis where it is essential that other than the normal spacing between lines be allowed. For tables, double-ruled lines should be separated by only a fractional portion of a normal space. In placing the superscripts for footnotes, the platen (or roll) must be rotated less than one space. By shifting the *line-space release*, it is possible to turn the platen freely, and when the release is again shifted to its original position, the material will be aligned as before. When one wishes to establish a new basal alignment, however, use of the *variable line-space device* will permit the new line to be fixed at the desired point. If a person is unfamiliar with the mechanics of a typewriter, he should carefully study a manual of directions for his machine, or ask an expert to show him how to do the many things of which it is capable.

Period leaders

• At various points in the thesis, for example, in large tables and on the pages containing the table of contents and the list of Figures, double-spaced periods (called "period leaders" by printers) are required. They must be so arranged that the periods will be aligned perpendicularly and will end at the same point on the right-hand side — usually about two or three spaces before the material to which the line guides the eye of the reader. A simple method of accomplishing this consists in placing all the periods on the even numbers of the typing scale found on all typewriters. This will eliminate the difficulty of much back-spacing or of guessing just where the first period should come in order to achieve uniformity and neatness of appearance.

Hyphens and dashes

• In typed material, a hyphen and a dash are made differently. A hyphen consists of one mark (-), whereas a dash consists of two marks (--). The following lines illustrate these points:

```
The stock-exchange list was short.
The stock--American Can--was selling above par.
```

It will be noted that *no space* precedes or follows either of these marks of punctuation — each is immediately preceded and followed by a typed letter, with no intervening space.

Proofreading

• The entire thesis should be proofread *before* going to the typist to have final copies made, and it should be read in its entirety by the writer *after the final copies have been typed*. The spelling of words unfamiliar to the student, as well as the syllabic division of words at the ends of lines, should be carefully checked by the student. It is impossible to place too great stress upon the necessity of having a scholarly product when the thesis is finally ready for the committee's consideration.

Expert typists are habituated to looking over each page before it is removed from the machine. At that time, it is possible to make a simple correction on all copies of the work so that it is hardly noticeable. If the papers are withdrawn from the typewriter before an error is corrected, each copy should be corrected separately, due care being taken to insure that the new letters are of about the same degree of darkness as the rest of the typing on the page.

Erasures and corrections

● Few universities refuse to accept a thesis containing a corrected error, but all of them insist that the number be kept to a minimum and that each be neatly accomplished.

Two ink erasers (one for large surfaces and one for tiny spots) and an erasing shield (either metal or plastic) are basic to all successful corrections. If the erasure is for the purpose of correcting an erroneous letter, the correct one should be struck once *before* the erasure is made; this will make the final product look better than otherwise it would. By selecting an opening in the eraser shield only slightly larger than the matter to be erased, by carefully handling the eraser, and by using a drop of ink-remover to dim the color left by the ribbon, a nearly clean space can be provided for the retyping. The letter to fill the erased space should be struck lightly, or the point of correction will be evident because of the heavier and darker impression of the corrected letter.

If the correction involves increasing by one the number of letters previously occupying a space, careful use of the back-spacer will allow distribution of the increase over several spaces. Simply crowding two letters together in the space meant for one is an undesirable practice, for it is virtually impossible to accomplish this without having an unsightly piece of work. Experience has shown that it is possible to retype a page of normal context in about the same time that it takes to make two or three minor corrections, or one major change, and the result is much more satisfactory.

Pen-and-ink corrections, whether in the form of changed letters, deleted letters or words, or added letters or words, are never permissible in a thesis. Either the errors should be corrected on the typewriter, or the page should be retyped.

Checking the final product

● After the thesis is completed, the student should check the entire work in an effort to locate any error in it. All numbers should be checked against the originals, and computations should be checked to guarantee absolute accuracy in the copies presented to the university. The entire text should be scanned for any possible mistake in grammar or rhetoric. The sequence of page numbers, the correspondence of captions and numbers of tables and Figures in the text and in the lists of tables and Figures, and the accuracy of page numbers in citations should be examined with care. In the bibliography, every title must be compared with the title-page of the volume or article listed. Many theses are not accepted because they contain errors that are obvious to a trained worker, errors that could easily have been corrected had proper precautions been taken in preparing the work for submission.

7 | MATTERS OF STYLE

THERE ARE SO MANY POINTS which deal with style and correctness in writing that no attempt will be made to include all of them, or even very many of them, in this manual. A few general guideposts, however, will be set up in this chapter to help the student avoid some of the more common pitfalls of writing and expression. The student should form the habit of refreshing his background from time to time by reading good handbooks of writing and rhetoric. Ease in writing and correctness of usage are attained only by constant study and practice. Careful scrutiny of each sentence and conscientious attention to every doubtful term or expression will develop habits of good English that will make each succeeding effort easier than the last. Having several standard reference books within easy reach will diminish the tendency to allow a question on correctness of form to go unanswered. The Bibliography, pages 68 to 70, lists several guides that will prove helpful.

Style of writing

● Many writers of theses tend to deprecate the importance of style in writing. Although they attach full importance to the research undertaken and the conclusions reached, they fail to put proper emphasis on the manner of reporting. Actually, the presentation is an integral part of the whole project. No matter how valuable a scholar's work, it becomes a contribution to the field of knowledge only when it is adequately communicated to others. The student must remember, therefore, that members of his thesis committee and other interested persons can learn of his particular contributions only when they are properly presented — in a word, there is no way around the importance of good writing.

A thesis is a formal presentation and should be written at the formal level of standard English. Colloquial and conversational modes of expression that are perfectly good usage in less formal writing are therefore inappropriate in a thesis.

A thesis must be accurate; therefore, its language must be accurate. If in addition to being accurate a thesis is made forceful, through proper emphasis of important points, so much the better. If in addition to being both accurate and forceful a thesis is presented with unity and coherence, and written in a charming style, the highest standard of expository writing will have been achieved. This level is seldom reached by thesis students, but any work submitted for a graduate degree should have at least the two qualities first mentioned: accuracy and force of expression. The suggestions offered in this chapter will help the student to present his findings accurately and forcefully. Skill in writing will be developed only after a period of practice in attending to details both of form and of expression. One-tenth talent and nine-tenths practice is a good formula for the development of an able writer.

Person

● Since a thesis is a report of an investigation conducted according to scientific principles and is not of a personal or conversational nature, it should be written in the third person. This means that the personal pronouns *I, we, you, me, my, our,* and *us* and direct commands will not appear except in quotations or in situations other than those involving the writer or the reader. Use of the third person requires some skill, but once the habit of writing in it has been acquired, it is easy to use.

This rule does not mean that the use of the first- and second-person pronouns is never to be sanctioned in formal writing. On the contrary, in a book or essay in which the personal experiences or opinions of the author have a definite place, it is entirely proper. But a thesis must be more than a report of personal experience or opinion — more than a compilation of materials and data. It must embody a critical analysis of the problem and of the evidence relating to that problem; and it is presumed to be scientifically so sound in its logic that, upon acquaintance with the evidence presented, the majority of qualified judges will agree that the writer's conclusions are valid. It is thus presumed to have a scientific impersonality that makes the use of the first- and second-person pronouns stylistically out of harmony with the function of the writing.

There are times when reference to the person who conducted the experiment or made the investigation is unavoidable. In such cases, the expressions "the experimenter" and "the investigator" are permissible. The student should bear in mind, however, that the demands of good taste and the possibility of confusion do not permit reference to "the author" or "the writer" when referring to the author of the thesis, unless it is made very clear that he is the one to whom reference is made. By judicious choice of words and proper arrangement of material, the entire thesis, with the exception of certain portions dealing with the technique of procedure, can be written without direct mention of the author.

Continued use of the impersonal "it" cannot be sanctioned. If the form of the sentence is reversed and the subject placed at the beginning — its logical position — the monotony resulting from repetition of the word "it" and the loss of force that comes from relegating key words to the predicate may be eliminated.

> *Weak.* It is clear that Vico's writings influenced the development of Michelet's thought.
>
> *Improved.* Vico's writings clearly influenced the development of Michelet's thought.

Tense
● Since a thesis recounts what has been done, the manuscript should be written in the past tense. This does not mean that the thesis writer may not use present-tense and future-tense forms; but when he does so, he should make it clear to the reader that the discussion in which these tenses are used has to do with what is true at the time of the reading or will be true in the future, and does not refer to what has already taken place. Frequent use of these tenses tends to give the impression that the thesis is merely a general discussion or an essay embodying the unsubstantiated opinions of the writer.

Spelling
● All words that appear in the thesis must be correctly spelled. Regular use of a standard dictionary will be helpful. For correct spelling of proper names, the student should refer to the best available authority. If there is doubt regarding the accuracy of the spelling of numerous words in the thesis, an expert accustomed to editing material for publication should be employed to correct it before final copies are typed.

Simplified spelling, for example, "enuf" for "enough" and "altho" for "although," should not be used except in direct quotations from another source.

Division of words
● The right-hand margin of a typed manuscript should be as even as is consistent with good practice in dividing words, but care should be exercised to avoid too many hyphens at the ends of lines. Rather than carry the division of words to an extreme, it is better to leave blank the last three to seven spaces at the end of a line.

When to avoid great marginal unevenness the division of a word is necessary, the break should come between two syllables. Even so, one-letter and two-letter divisions, such as e-vil, a-tone, en-veloper, entire-ly, consecrat-ed, are not acceptable.

The word should be written on one line, or another division point used; for example, envel-oper, conse-crated. As a general rule, compound words should be divided according to their major parts, e.g., "un-even" rather than "une-ven," "volley-ball" rather than "vol-leyball."

It is good practice to refer to a dictionary or an approved manual of style when dividing all but the most common words, for improper word-divisions can cause the reader to suspect that the writer may be careless on major points as well as minor ones. Foreign words, in particular, should be carefully checked for proper syllabification.

It is preferable, except where impractical in the case of very long names, to write both given name and surname, or initials and surname, on the same line. Letters of a radio station or government agency, the name of the month and the day, parts of an equation, and combinations of monetary expressions, dates, and hour of the day should never be divided and run over to a second line. The following are examples:

KWLZ $\quad\quad$ RFC $\quad$ March 2 $\quad$ $6x + 4y = 27$

$C + O_2 \longrightarrow CO_2$ $\quad$ \$1,378.50 $\quad$ 525 B.C. $\quad$ 4:00 A.M.

Very long formulas or equations may be set on lines by themselves, if necessary, to avoid breaking. If an equation is so long and complex that it must unavoidably be run over to another line, the break should come if possible before the equality sign (algebraic equations) or after the arrow (chemical equations).

Abbreviations

● Accepted standards of thesis style usually prohibit the use of abbreviations in the text of the thesis (except Mr., Messrs., Mrs., and their foreign equivalents; Dr., St., Rev., and Hon., preceding proper names; and Esq., Sr., and Jr. following proper names). In some technical theses, accepted abbreviations such as 16 mm., 250 cc., and 5 ft. 11 in. are permitted. All other words should, in the straight context, be spelled out in full.

This rule does not hold for material included in footnotes, appendixes, bibliographies, and, most particularly, in tables, where abbreviations are not only permissible but desirable, and where standards of thesis form, especially in the sciences and mathematics, allow exceedingly abbreviated forms to be used. A student should ascertain from the chairman of his thesis committee the extent to which abbreviations may be used in his particular case.

Capitalization

● Standard practice in the matter of capitalization of words in both English and other languages should be followed. In most cases, a good dictionary will serve as a guide; in questionable cases, the student should refer to a manual of style, such as one of those listed in the Bibliography, page 69.

Enumeration of items

● It is often desirable to enumerate items so as to attract special attention to their number or to the relationship that exists between them. The following are standard procedures for the three commoner cases:

Rule 1. When the numbered or lettered items are so brief that they can be woven easily into the text, the figures or letters should be enclosed in parentheses:

Wrong. `The activities of the company are divided into three categories: 1. management, 2. promotion and sales, and 3. operations and maintenance.`

Right. `The activities of the company are divided into three categories: (1) management, (2) promotion and sales, and (3) operations and maintenance.`

Rule 2. When, because of the length of the items or for some other reason, it is desirable to enumerate in tabular form items that do not have subdivisions, the parentheses are eliminated. Either letters or numerals may be used, although common practice is to employ Arabic numerals.

```
1. Organization and outline of the problem.
2. Description of the experimental technique.
3. Presentation of the findings under suit-
      able headings, together with tabular
      materials necessary to substantiate the
      points made.
```

Rule 3. When the items are in outline form, with subdivisions, the enumeration should show the relationship between them by indention and the following use of numerals and letters:

```
 I. Under the head of . . . .
     A. Under . . . .
         1. Under . . . .
             a) Under . . . .
                 (1) Under . . . .
                     (a) Under . . . .
                             i) Under . . . .
                            ii) Under . . . .
                     (b) Under . . . .
                 (2) Under . . . .
             b) Under . . . .
         2. Under . . . .
     B. Under . . . .
II. Under . . . .
```

Use of numbers

• Theses filled with numbers may confuse the reader unless the writer adheres strictly to the rules regarding their use. Above all else, the manner of presenting numerical data must be consistent throughout the thesis.

In a thesis containing few numbers, all of them should be spelled out.

Numbers less than one hundred and round numbers are usually spelled out. Numbers larger than one hundred, except round numbers, are usually given in figures. If, however, in referring to the same series there are numbers both smaller and larger than one hundred, figures are used for all of them. (See Examples 1, 2, 4, and 5, page 65.)

A fraction is always spelled out, unless it is part of a large number; for example, one-half, but 296$\frac{1}{2}$.

No sentence should begin with a numeral. Rearrangement of the words will usually allow the number to be placed within the sentence so that numerals may be used. When the number must come at the beginning of the sentence, however, it should be spelled out, even if later numbers are given in figures. (See Example 4, page 65.)

If there are two series of numbers, whether or not both series contain large and small numbers, one series may be spelled out and the other given numerically. (See Example 5, page 65.)

Numbers with four or more digits, except street, telephone, and page numbers and dates, must have commas inserted to point off thousands and millions. No space is left after a comma used in this way. (See Examples 2 and 3, page 65.) In dates, B.C. ("before Christ"), if used, follows the year; A.D. (*anno Domini*, "in the year of our Lord") precedes it.

Percentages are usually given in Arabic numerals, although these may be smaller than one hundred. The words "per" and "cent" are not linked together as one word. They need not be underscored, despite their Latin origin (*per centum*), nor need terminal punctuation be used to indicate abbreviation. The symbol % should not be used, except in certain technical theses where proper authority indicates that the practice is standard. (See Example 7, below.)

Contextual reference to numbers taken from tables should be in the form of numerals and not spelled out even if the number is small. (See Example 8, below.)

The following examples illustrate the proper use of numbers:

Example 1. The survey covered ninety-seven college newspapers and one thousand high school publications of various kinds.

Example 2. Built in 1916, the elementary school at 10916 Main Street had a play area comprising 4,729 square feet of concrete and 57,128 square feet of grass.

Example 3. A comparison of the two illustrations on page 1078 suggests that there was little change in agricultural methods between 1900 B.C. and A.D. 1400.

Example 4. Forty-five of the 517 men were Indians, of whom 7 were chiefs.

Example 5. In the contest, the total for ten of the participants was $498\frac{1}{2}$ points, while the total for the remaining five hundred sixteen participants was only $27\frac{1}{2}$ points.

Example 6. Family troubles accounted for one-sixth of the absenteeism, and illness for one-fourth of it, but more than one-half of the absenteeism was still left unexplained. BUT: One half of the group was inoculated; the other half served as a control.

Example 7. When a count was made, it was found that 37 per cent of those registered had voted.

Example 8. Table I shows that only 22 tests were run.

Punctuation

● Throughout the thesis, in the body of the manuscript, in the footnotes, in the bibliography, and in the appendix, it is essential that the accepted rules for punctuation be followed. There are certain places where thesis form requires a special application of a rule, but there is no place where thesis form violates the usage established by authorities.

Whenever quotations are made, if they are short enough to be included in a double-spaced portion of the manuscript, ordinarily not more than three lines in length, the quoted material is enclosed in quotation marks, and the footnote reference number is placed outside the quotation marks. In long quotations, ordinarily more than three lines in length, the quotation marks are not used, but the material is indented four spaces on the left and is single-spaced, thus indicating that the material is taken directly from some outside source.

Punctuation check list

● Although no attempt will be made here to give all the rules of punctuation that a student should follow, the rules that are most commonly violated by writers will be listed, so that the writer of a thesis may check against them. A student who makes many errors in writing should consult a handbook of English and use it constantly during the preparation of his work.

Rule 1. A period should be placed after every complete declarative or imperative sentence. There is a possibility that two such sentences may, without undue breach of good form, be linked together by a semicolon; but the use of a comma instead of a period constitutes what is known as a "comma fault" or "comma blunder."

Wrong. Lee was well aware of the dangers of his position, he took steps, therefore, to reinforce his exposed right wing.

Right. Lee was well aware of the dangers of his position. He took steps, therefore, to reinforce his exposed right wing.

Right. Lee was well aware of the dangers of his position; he took steps, therefore, to reinforce his exposed right wing.

Rule 2. A period should not be placed before any part of a sentence that is merely a concluding member of that sentence, for example, a participial phrase, an appositive, or a subordinate clause.

Wrong. A thesis consists of a report of a scientific investigation. Together with a review of the pertinent literature.

Right. A thesis consists of a report of a scientific investigation, together with a review of the pertinent literature.

Wrong. Mendel began his famous experiments with garden peas. While he was teaching science at Brunn.

Right. Mendel began his famous experiments with garden peas while he was teaching science at Brunn.

Rule 3. A comma is used to separate co-ordinate clauses of a compound sentence when they are joined by one of the pure co-ordinating conjunctions (*but, for, or, nor*). When the conjunction is omitted, a semicolon, rather than a comma, is used. Writers differ on the question of punctuation to accompany the conjunction *and*. Many now omit the comma preceding it.

Wrong. It is not unethical to press every advantage but only admissible testimony should be offered to the court.

Right. It is not unethical to press every advantage, but only admissible testimony should be offered to the court.

Right. An administrative officer should equalize the loads carried by the men in his department; he should note their individual differences.

Wrong. The sample was not representative, therefore the conclusions were valueless.

Right. The sample was not representative; therefore, the conclusions were valueless.

Rule 4. A comma should be placed before a nonrestrictive relative clause, and at the end of such a clause if the end of the clause is not also the end of the sentence. A nonrestrictive relative clause is one that may be omitted without spoiling the meaning of the main clause of the sentence. It is included for purposes of explanation.

Incidentally, it should be observed that the relative pronoun *that* is generally employed to introduce restrictive clauses only, while *which* is employed for nonrestrictive clauses. However, if another *that* closely precedes the restrictive clause, euphony sometimes makes it preferable to substitute *which* for the relative *that*. The relative *who* is used both restrictively and nonrestrictively.

Wrong. Lilies, that fester, smell far worse than weeds.

Right. Lilies that fester smell far worse than weeds.

Wrong. The atomic nucleus which is one-trillionth the size of an atom is the innermost known limit of matter.

Right. The atomic nucleus, which is one-trillionth the size of an atom, is the innermost known limit of matter.

Right. Children, who are not "miniature adults," should not be measured by adult standards.

Right. Children who do not make friends easily need help in group situations.

Rule 5. Commas should be placed around a word or brief phrase used parenthetically.

Wrong. He did not however know that the theory had been disproved.

Right. He did not, however, know that the theory had been disproved.

Wrong. Nast the leading cartoonist of his day attacked political corruption.

Right. Nast, the leading cartoonist of his day, attacked political corruption.

Rule 6. When a subordinate clause precedes an independent clause of a sentence, a comma should be placed between them. This is usually not done when the subordinate clause follows the independent clause.

> *Wrong.* Because he was awkward and shy the other children made fun of him.
> *Right.* Because he was awkward and shy, the other children made fun of him.

Rule 7. Best usage places a comma before the conjunction of a series of the form a, b, and c.

> *Wrong.* The school offers courses in economics, education and history.
> *Right.* The school offers courses in economics, education, and history.

Rule 8. The use of quotation marks in connection with other marks of punctuation may be covered by three rules:

First, a comma or a period is always, under all circumstances, placed inside the final quotation marks.

> *Wrong.* "The best ideas", says Seneca, "are common property".
> *Right.* "The best ideas," says Seneca, "are common property."

Secondly, a semicolon or a colon should always follow the quotation marks.

> *Wrong.* The band played "America;" the ceremony was over.
> *Right.* The band played "America"; the ceremony was over.

Thirdly, in the case of a question mark or an exclamation mark, the quotation marks follow the other mark if it belongs to that portion of the sentence enclosed by the quotation marks. Otherwise, the quotation marks precede the exclamation mark or question mark.

> *Wrong.* Did he say, "I resign?"
> *Right.* Did he say, "I resign"?
> *Wrong.* He asked, "May I come in"?
> *Right.* He asked, "May I come in?"

The hyphen

● The hyphen is an extremely troublesome mark of punctuation. Its position may change the meaning of an entire expression. When a hyphen is used in any but the commonest phrases, the whole should be examined carefully to make certain that the meaning is what is intended. Where there is ambiguity, an oral reading in which the words joined by the hyphen are spoken close together with a pause before the next word will usually settle any question regarding the position of the hyphen. For example, there is a vast difference between the meanings of the expressions "Australian-ballot controversy" and "Australian ballot-controversy." The proper position of the hyphen in terms of meaning may easily be judged if the expression is read aloud.

The commonest use for the hyphen is to join two or more words used as an attributive adjective before a noun, as in the following example:

The man-eating shark infests the waters of the South Seas.

Consistency

● Throughout this manual, an effort has been made to stress the fact that the student must be consistent in everything that he does. Although one form may be superior to another, or either of two forms may be superior to a third, the student must be consistent in using the form that he has selected and chooses to follow.

BIBLIOGRAPHY

Allbutt, Sir Thomas Clifford. *Notes on the Composition of Scientific Papers.* 3rd ed. New York: The Macmillan Company, 1923. 192 pp.

The Amos Tuck School of Administration and Finance, Dartmouth College. *Manual on Research and Reports.* New York: McGraw-Hill Book Company, Inc., 1937. 140 pp.

Especially applies to investigations in the social sciences.

Cole, Arthur H., and Karl W. Bigelow. *A Manual of Thesis-Writing.* New York: John Wiley and Sons, Inc., 1934. 28 pp.

Prepared especially for the use of undergraduates working in the field of social science. A convenient compilation of rules and usages helpful in the preparation of scientific papers.

Cunningham, W. K., Jr., and Ben M. Patrick. *Typing Academic Papers.* Durham, North Carolina: Duke University Press, 1937. 118 pp.

A manual and a model for the author and typist.

Dissertations in History and English. University of Iowa Studies, No. 183. Iowa City, Iowa: University of Iowa, July 15, 1930. 30 pp.

An outline of the procedure to be followed in preparing theses and dissertations in the departments of history and English.

Duke Mathematical Journal: Author's Manual. Durham, North Carolina: Duke University Press, [n.d.]. 18 pp.

While the booklet deals specifically with directions on preparation of papers for publication in the *Duke Mathematical Journal*, the form suggested is commonly used in the general field of mathematics.

Long, John A. *Conducting and Reporting Research in Education.* Bulletin No. 6 of the Department of Educational Research. Toronto, Canada: University of Toronto, 1936. 77 pp.

Modern Language Association of America. *The MLA Style Sheet.* Compiled by William Riley Parker. New York: The Modern Language Association of America, 100 Washington Square East, New York 3, N.Y., 1951. 32 pp.

The instructions given are more or less official for forty-six journals, most of them in the field of languages. The emphasis is on manuscript, rather than thesis, preparation; but it is a helpful guide.

Price, Miles O. *A Practical Manual of Standard Legal Citations.* New York: Oceana Publications, 1950. 106 pp.

Publication Manual of the American Psychological Association. Washington, D.C.: American Psychological Association, 1952. 61 pp.

Reeder, Ward G. *How to Write a Thesis.* Bloomington, Illinois: Public School Publishing Company, 1930. 216 pp.

A brief and useful treatment of the mechanics of thesis preparation with exceptional fullness of detail. An earlier edition is just as useful and more concise.

Royal Society. *General Notes on the Preparation of Scientific Papers.* London: Cambridge University Press, 1950. 26 pp.

Intended primarily for the use of persons preparing scientific papers for publication, this pamphlet contains many helpful suggestions for specific fields in the sciences.

Trelease, Sam Farlow. *The Scientific Paper: How to Prepare It, How to Write It.* 2d ed. Baltimore: The Williams and Wilkins Company, 1951. 163 pp.

Although most helpful to writers of theses in the sciences, this book will also prove helpful to anyone engaged in preparing a research paper, particularly one that involves tables, charts, and illustrations. An earlier version is *The Preparation of Scientific Papers*, by Sam Farlow Trelease and E. S. Yule, in numerous editions.

Turabian, Kate L. *A Manual for Writers of Dissertations.* Chicago: The University of Chicago Press, 1937. 61 pp.

This booklet is based on the *Style Manual* of the University of Chicago Press and is directed specifically to the preparation of dissertations in the University of Chicago. It will be helpful, in many ways, to any thesis writer.

LANGUAGE USAGE

Ball, Alice Morton. *Compounding in the English Language.* New York: The H. W. Wilson Company, 1941. 226 pp.

The standard work on spelling and hyphenation, as well as special uses of words. Other style books usually have a short section dealing with this same subject.

Foerster, Norman, and J. M. Steadman, Jr. *Writing and Thinking.* 5th ed.; revised by James B. McMillan. Boston: Houghton Mifflin Company, 1952. 448 pp.

Fowler, H. W. *A Dictionary of Modern English Usage.* Oxford: Clarendon Press, 1926. 742 pp.

Greever, Garland, and Easley S. Jones. *The Century Handbook of Writing.* 4th ed. New York: D. Appleton-Century Company, Inc., 1942. 348+364 pp.

Handbook for English 102. 3d preliminary ed. Chicago: University of Chicago Bookstore, 1933. 81 pp.

A handbook designed for a course in composition in which much time is devoted to the preparation of research papers.

Manly, John Matthews, and Edith Rickert. *The Writer's Index of Good Form and Good English.* New York: Henry Holt and Company, 1923. 261 pp.

A valuable handbook for the writer to have on his desk.

A Manual of Style. 11th ed. Chicago: The University of Chicago Press, 1949. 497 pp.

Contains typographical rules governing the publications of the University of Chicago, together with specimens of type.

Mawson, C. O. S. (ed.). *Roget's International Thesaurus of English Words and Phrases: A Complete Book of Synonyms and Antonyms.* New York: Thomas Y. Crowell Company, 1940. 857 pp.

The chief reference on synonyms and antonyms, embodying Roget's original work with numerous additions and modernizations.

Perrin, Porter G. *Writer's Guide and Index to English.* Revised edition. Chicago: Scott, Foresman and Company, 1950. 834 pp.

Skillin, Marjorie E., Robert M. Gay, and others. *Words into Type.* New York: Appleton-Century-Crofts, Inc., 1948. 585 pp.

The purport of this book is to help authors prepare for publication, but the instructions contained therein will be of value to writers of theses whether to be published or not.

United States Government Printing Office. *U.S. Government Style Manual.* Revised edition, January, 1953. Washington, D.C.: Government Printing Office, 1953. 492 pp.

The guide followed by the Government Printing Office, one of the largest publishers in the world. The forms there set forth are required in all Government publications and are followed by many others.

Wood, George McLane. *Suggestions to Authors of Papers Submitted for Publication by the United States Geological Survey.* 4th ed.; revised by Bernard H. Lane. United States Department of the Interior; Washington, D.C.: Government Printing Office, 1935. 126 pp.

Although designed to aid in the preparation of papers in geology, this government publication contains excellent sections on form to be used in a manuscript and detailed suggestions as to expression.

Woolley, Edwin C., and Franklin W. Scott. *College Handbook of Composition.* 5th ed.; revised by Frederick Bracher. Boston: D. C. Heath and Company, 1951. 344 pp.

RESEARCH

Abelson, Harold H. *The Art of Educational Research.* Yonkers, N.Y.: World Book Company, 1933. 332 pp.

A useful volume in which scientific research and educational practice are effectively combined.

Almack, John C. *Research and Thesis Writing.* Boston: Houghton Mifflin Company, 1930. 310 pp.

A textbook on the principles and techniques of thesis construction for the use of graduate students in universities and colleges, dealing in the main with methods of research.

Good, Carter V., A. S. Barr, and Douglas E. Scates. *Methodology of Educational Research.* New York: Appleton-Century-Crofts, Inc., 1938. 882 pp.

A comprehensive work dealing with methods of research and presentation of research findings, especially in the field of education.

Hockett, Homer Carey. *Introduction to Research in American History.* 2d ed. New York: The Macmillan Company, 1950. 179 pp.

An excellent guide for the beginner in historical research, stressing the essential procedures in this field.

Morize, André. *Problems and Methods of Literary History.* Boston: Ginn and Company, 1922. 314 pp.

Intended for French majors and drawing its illustrations from French literature, but with the principles and the details of the illustrations so explained that it is easily usable by students of English and other literature. There is no parallel work using English illustrations. Indispensable for students specializing in literature.

Seyfried, John Edward. *Principles and Mechanics of Research.* The University of New Mexico Bulletin, No. 269. Albuquerque, New Mexico: The University of New Mexico Press, 1935. 240 pp.

Emphasis on term reports and theses.

LISTS OF APPROVED ABBREVIATIONS IN CITING JOURNALS

Education Index List of Periodicals Indexed. New York: The H. W. Wilson Company, 1952.

List of Periodicals Abstracted by Chemical Abstracts. Columbus, Ohio: American Chemical Society, 1951.

Publication Manual of the American Psychological Association. Washington, D.C.: American Psychological Association (1333 16th Street N.W.), 1952. Pp. 48–51.

Style Manual. New York: American Institute of Physics, 1951.

Wood, George McLane. *Suggestions to Authors of Papers Submitted for Publication by the United States Geological Survey.* 4th ed.; revised by Bernard H. Lane. United States Department of the Interior; Washington, D.C.: Government Printing Office, 1935. Pp. 19–29.

APPENDIX:
SPECIMEN FORMS

● The following facsimile pages illustrate matters of form and placement of materials discussed in the body of the text. In a thesis, of course, the page is typewritten on one side only.

SPECIAL GUIDE SHEET

(See page 57 for instructions on how to use.)

1
2
3
4
5
6
7
8
9
10
11
12
13
14
15
16
17
18
19
20
21
22
23
24
25

10
9
8
7
6
5
4
3
2
1

(11 single spaces
from top of page)

A DISCRIMINATIVE STUDY OF METHODS FOR THE QUANTITATIVE

DETERMINATION OF FLUORINE

(5 single spaces)

(6 single spaces)

A Dissertation

Presented to

the Faculty of the Graduate School

Leland Stanford Junior University

(5 single spaces)

(6 single spaces)

In Partial Fulfillment

of the Requirements for the Degree

Doctor of Philosophy

(5 single spaces)

(3 single spaces)

by

William Robert Howard

June 1953

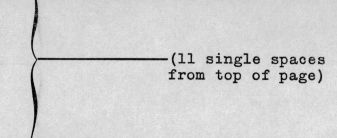

(11 single spaces
from top of page)

AN ANALYSIS OF THE INFLUENCE OF RALPH WALDO EMERSON

ON WALT WHITMAN

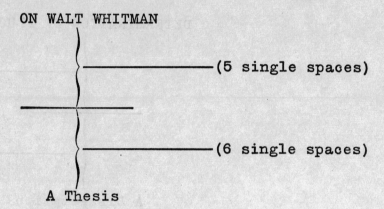

(5 single spaces)

(6 single spaces)

A Thesis

Presented to

the Faculty of the Department of English

University of Wisconsin

(5 single spaces)

(6 single spaces)

In Partial Fulfillment

of the Requirements for the Degree

Master of Arts

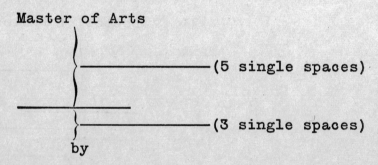

(5 single spaces)

(3 single spaces)

by

Mary Alice Armstrong

June 1952

(10 single spaces
from top of page)

A COMPARATIVE INVESTIGATION OF THE BEHAVIOR OF

STUDENTS UNDER AN HONOR SYSTEM AND A PROCTOR

SYSTEM IN THE SAME UNIVERSITY

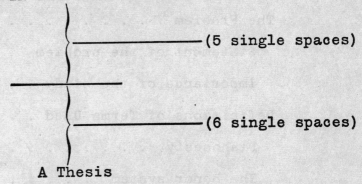

(5 single spaces)

(6 single spaces)

A Thesis

Presented to

the Faculty of the School of Education

The University of Southern California

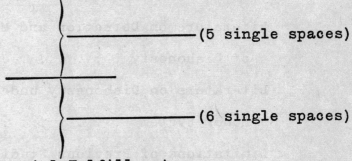

(5 single spaces)

(6 single spaces)

In Partial Fulfillment

of the Requirements for the Degree

Master of Science in Education

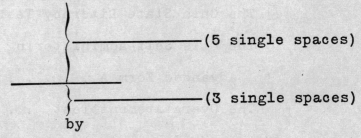

(5 single spaces)

(3 single spaces)

by

John Clarence Porter

August 1953

[77]

TABLE OF CONTENTS

LIST OF TABLES

LIST OF FIGURES

CHAPTER I

THE PROBLEM AND DEFINITIONS OF TERMS USED

For many years a difference of opinion has existed regarding the relative effectiveness of the honor system and the proctor system as means of eliminating dishonesty during the taking of examinations. The majority of the claims made by the proponents of the two systems have been based upon limited observation, and in no instance has experimental evidence been presented to support the contentions of either side.

I. THE PROBLEM

Statement of the problem. It was the purpose of this study (1) to compare the honesty, in certain specific situations, of university students under an honor system and a proctor system in the same institution; (2) to show the relation between trustworthiness in these situations and such factors as age, intelligence, sex, scholarship, and total number of years of schooling; and (3) to present student attitudes with regard to honesty, as revealed through a questionnaire study.

Importance of the study. Character development has frequently been stressed as one of the most important aims

of education. In spite, however, of the rather general
recognition by schoolmen of personality and character objec-
tives and the use of many techniques designed to aid in the
attainment of these goals, tools for measuring the effects
of moral education have been few and inadequate. Especially
limited have been those tests of the actual behavior of the
individual in an ethical situation. Pencil-and-paper tests
on which the subject expresses judgments on moral situations
occur most frequently among the available tools. The limitations of these have been pointed out by Bronner; information, rather than moral conduct, is tested.[1] In this study
an attempt was made to employ techniques of which the above
criticism cannot be made.

II. DEFINITIONS OF TERMS USED

Dishonesty. Dishonest conduct was interpreted as
meaning the intentional taking, accepting, or keeping, by an
individual, of anything not rightfully belonging to him, as
well as violation of trust, lack of integrity, of fraudulent
misrepresentation. Since, furthermore, intent was almost
impossible to discover except as it expressed itself in
conduct, the subjects were given the benefit of any doubt

---

[1]A. F. Bronner, "The Apperceptive Abilities of De-
linquents," Journal of Delinquency, VII (January, 1922), 43-
54. [Or, 7:43-54, January, 1922.]

and were assumed to be honest unless they were found to be guilty of clearly dishonest conduct.

The honor system. Throughout the report of this investigation, the term "honor system" shall be interpreted as meaning the plan that had been in use at the University for nearly thirty years when the original experiment was performed. Under it, the student, upon entering school, was required to sign a pledge neither to give nor to accept aid on any of his school work and to report any violations of the code of honor that came to his attention. At the end of each examination he was required to sign a statement to the effect that he had complied with the code of honor while taking the examination.

The proctor system. Since this experiment was conducted in only one university, the term "proctor system" shall be interpreted as indicating the plan specified for that particular school. The institution required the instructor to administer his own examinations and to remain in the room to reduce, as much as possible, the amount of cheating. When the class was exceptionally large, the instructor was supposed to secure the aid of student assistants or tutors to help in proctoring the group. It may

(This is only a portion of a chapter, included to give an idea of how thesis material would be presented, and is not to be considered as being complete in any respect.)

CHAPTER II

REVIEW OF THE LITERATURE

Much has been written in regard to the prevalence of deceptive behavior, the incidence and causes of delinquency and criminality, and the mental traits of moral deviators; but only a brief summary of the work done on problems very closely related to the one at hand will here be given.

I. LITERATURE ON DETECTION AND MEASUREMENT
OF DISHONESTY

Voelker, in attempting to measure the effect of Boy Scout training on various phases of behavior, directly approached the problem of the detection of dishonesty when he tested eleven groups of boys in a series of specific situations. Various opportunities to overstate the extent of their knowledge were offered.[1] As a result, he said, "The results of the experiment do not warrant the general conclusion that it is unnecessary to train children in the formation of specific habits of morality."[2]

---

[1]Paul F. Voelker, The Function of Attitudes and Ideals in Social Education (Teachers College Contributions to Education, No. 112. New York: Teachers College, Columbia University, 1921), p. 86. [Material within parentheses may, at the discretion of the department, be omitted.]

[2]Ibid., p. 123.

14

Bird devised an ingenious method for the detection of cheating on objective examinations. Using a large class of students in an introductory course in psychology, he made exhaustive calculations to show the large number of identical errors caused by the author of one paper copying from a second paper. Four students were believed to have copied from papers belonging to their neighbors. The numbers of identical errors in the four pairs were 17, 25, 28, and 31, while the mean number of identical errors between a cheater's paper and twenty papers chosen at random was 4. The mean number of identical errors found in one hundred pairs of papers chosen at random was 4.35.[3] This was a new attack on the problem. Bird reported that:

> These comparisons enabled us to report the delinquent students to the Students' Work Committee. This committee considered the quantitative records to be irrefutable and did not at any time raise questions which concerned the accuracy of the proctors' observation. All four of the accused students denied dishonesty, but three quickly confessed guilt when confronted with the evidence, while one, whose paper showed twenty-eight identical errors, maintained innocence. Nevertheless, the committee unanimously convicted him.[4]

The marked degree of correlation between deceptive behavior and the tendency for a person to overstate the

---

[3] Charles Bird, "The Detection of Cheating in Objective Examinations," School and Society, XXV (February, 1927), 261. [Or, 25:261, February, 1927.]

[4] Ibid.

extent of his information was pointed out by both Voelker
and Raubenheimer. The latter found this definite inclina-
tion toward exaggeration on the part of thirty per cent of
his subjects.[5] The methods of these authors, although based
on objective data, lack the statistical accuracy inherent in
those of Bird.[6]

Hartshorne and May have done valuable work in
devising tests of character traits and in revealing the
social attitudes of different groups. They have succeeded,
after many trials, in constructing a series of pencil-and-
paper tests that they insist will measure certain phases of
character. The misconduct includes securing assistance when
one is not supposed to, stealing money from the material
used in a puzzle or test, cheating in various parlor games
or contests, and other violations of trust. While the cor-
relations secured between moral knowledge as measured and
actual deception as observed in the experimental situations
were not high, Hartshorne and May seem to have uncovered
usable measures of the components of character.[7]

---

[5]Voelker, op. cit., p. 80; A. S. Raubenheimer, "An
Experimental Study of Some Behavior Traits in the Poten-
tially Delinquent Boy," Psychological Monographs, XXXIV
(May, 1925), 1-107. [Or, 34:1-107, May, 1925.]

[6]Bird, loc. cit.

[7]H. Hartshorne and M. A. May, Studies in Deceit
(New York: The Macmillan Company, 1928), 432 pp.

TABLE III

ANALYSIS OF JANITORIAL SERVICES, PASADENA CITY SCHOOLS, 1948-1949

School plant	Square feet of floor space	Number of rooms	Number of janitors	Total salaries of janitors	Total janitors' supplies	Cost per 1000 sq. ft. per annum
Altadena	32,080	35	1.75	$2,277.29	$100.62	$74.12
Arroyo Seco	10,996	14	1.00	1,565.95	23.56	144.55
Cleveland	23,481	26	1.00	1,678.56	78.25	74.82
Columbia	20,927	14	1.00	1,696.55	77.83	84.79
Edison	22,358	29	1.37	1,673.50	101.16	79.37
Emerson	51,587	42	1.63	2,397.35	86.71	48.15
Fremont	13,358	14	1.00	1,381.68	62.52	108.11
Garfield	33,027	31	1.00	1,764.01	82.83	55.92
Grant	48,937	34	1.50	2,135.34	215.84	48.04
Hamilton	21,311	23	1.37	1,702.50	168.01	87.77
Jackson	34,030	34	2.00	3,344.51	88.02	100.87
Jefferson	80,204	68	3.00	4,672.34	199.50	60.74
Lincoln	35,645	27	2.00	3,197.50	48.53	64.33
Linda Vista	8,403	12	1.00	737.32	36.14	92.04
Longfellow	63,569	55	2.50	3,625.06	192.75	60.06
Madison	58,355	49	2.00	3,298.50	149.20	59.10
McKinley	49,631	48	2.00	3,506.56	149.03	73.65
Roosevelt	21,056	24	1.00	250.00	5.74	12.15
San Rafael	16,345	19	1.00	758.51	55.97	49.83
Serra	23,910	26	1.00	1,702.78	51.26	73.36
Washington	43,903	49	2.37	3,652.88	215.02	88.10
Webster	22,955	22	1.37	2,042.00	172.29	96.46
Totals	736,068	695	33.86	$49,060.69	$2,360.78	$74.38 Aver.

The following incomplete paragraph is supplied to give the beginning thesis student some idea of how the contents of a table may be discussed in the context. At this point, he should review the instructions on page 46 on how to relate the table to the text.

The data with regard to grade-placement of pupils in relation to their ability as measured on the Stanford Test are presented in Table V. While there is a general tendency for the data to go from lower-left to upper-right, as they should, there is also a noticeable tendency for the columns to become longer as one reads from left to right. This means that there is a greater spread of ability in the higher grades than in the lower. In fact, although in Grade 2A there is a spread of only two years on the Stanford norm, in Grade 6B there is a spread of five and one-half years. This means that those barely capable of meeting fifth-grade requirements are in the same class with others capable of doing work on the level of the senior high school. The last two lines in the table, the medians and norms for all grades, indicate that, on the average, the pupils of Littletown are not retarded. Comparison with Table I, page 12, and Table VII, page 67, will indicate other factors that need to be taken into consideration as solutions to the situation are investigated. . . .

TABLE V

GRADE-PLACEMENT IN THE JEFFERSON SCHOOL, LITTLETOWN, ARIZONA, 1952-1953, AS COMPARED WITH THE NORMS FOR THE STANFORD COMPOSITE SCORE

Grade-placement	Littletown Grade								
	2A	3B	3A	4B	4A	5B	5A	6B	6A
Stanford norm									
10.0								1	
9.5-9.9									
9.0-9.4									1
8.5-8.9							1	1	1
8.0-8.4								5	4
7.5-7.9							1	8	3
7.0-7.4				1		2	9	14	8
6.5-6.9				1	1	5	11	12	8
6.0-6.4				1	2	14	9	14	5
5.5-5.9				3	7	19	19	7	5
5.0-5.4				8	10	11	7	2	2
4.5-4.9		2	1	19	11	22	3		
4.0-4.4		3	8	28	5	7			
3.5-3.9	1	12	15	6					
3.0-3.4	16	34	18	4		1			
2.5-2.9	29	15	3						
2.4	8								
Total	54	66	45	71	36	81	60	64	37
Median	2.83	3.27	3.68	4.46	5.1	5.48	6.06	6.87	7.03
Norm	2.7	3.2	3.7	4.2	4.7	5.2	5.7	6.2	6.7

NOTE: This table should be read as follows: Twenty-nine 2A Littletown pupils had grade-placements of from grade 2.5 to grade 2.9 on the Stanford composite norm; fifteen 3B pupils and three 3A pupils were similarly placed.

TABLE VI

PERCENTAGE OF STUDENTS OVER AGE, OF NORMAL AGE, AND UNDER AGE IN VARIOUS CALIFORNIA HIGH SCHOOLS, MARCH, 1952

Cities	Percentage over age	Percentage normal age	Percentage under age	Average years over age
Sacramento . . .	29.4	44.3	26.3	1.022
Glendale	31.9*	42.3	25.8	1.107
Berkeley	32.1	39.9	28.0	1.022
Oakland.	32.1	44.1	23.8	1.013
Pasadena	34.7	45.0	20.3	1.179
San Diego. . . .	35.2	41.2	23.6	1.041
Los Angeles. . .	35.9	40.6	23.5	1.117
San Francisco. .	36.0	43.0	21.0	1.216
Santa Monica . .	36.2	43.0	20.8	1.069
Long Beach . . .	36.9	43.6	19.5	1.132
Fresno	38.2	40.9	20.9	1.236
San Jose	38.6	38.2	23.2	1.188
Alhambra	38.9	38.8	22.3	1.102
Santa Ana. . . .	39.8	37.5	22.6	1.306
Santa Barbara. .	39.9	39.0	21.2	1.213
San Bernardino .	41.9	38.4	19.7	1.224

*This figure was computed on the basis of the nearest birthday of the pupil, whereas all other figures are in terms of age to the nearest whole month.

TABLE X

NUMBERS AND PERCENTAGES OF SUBJECTS WHO CHEATED ON EXAMINATIONS, BY CLASS, IN GROUPS A AND B

CLASS	GROUP A			GROUP B		
	Total no. of cases	Number who cheated	Per cent who cheated	Total no. of cases	Number who cheated	Per cent who cheated
Fresh.	31	4	13	63	26	41
Soph.	52	14	27	50	17	34
Jr.	77	35	45	59	33	56
Sr.	27	15	55	20	3	15
Grad.	3	2	67	13	3	23

| | SUBJECT | | | SEAT | | GRADES | | | | OTIS TEST | | | | | BOOK LIST | | | SPY SYSTEM | | | | | OVE |
Case Number	Age	Sex	Class	Seat Row	Seat Number	Course Grade	University Grade	Changed	Added	Marked Wrong	Error in Total	True Score	Number Checked	Fictitious	Case 1H	Case 2H	Case 3H	2-2	2-0	2-	1-2	1-0	
CLASS #1.																							
1	19	M	Fr.	4	5	3.3	2.8					45											
2	19	F	Fr.	1	2	3.3	3.3					33	19					9	5	1	2	3	0
3	17	F	Fr.	1	4	1.0	1.0					38	12					5	9	0	1	4	2
4	22	M	Jr.	1	7	2.7	1.5					37	12					11	6	0	9	2	6
5	20	M	Jr.	1	6	5.0	4.9					54	22					26	6	0	1	1	0
6	19	F	So.	1	8	2.0	2.6	1				42	13										
7	19	F	Fr.	1	9	1.0	1.0	1				37	18					5	5	0	10	5	4
8	21	M	Fr.	1	10	3.3	3.0					50	23					16	7	0	6	7	0
9	17	F	Fr.	1	11	2.0	2.0					36											
10	19	F	Fr.	2	1	1.0	1.0	(E corrected)				33	15					10	8	0	3	3	0
11	18	F	Fr.	2	3	2.0	2.0					42	18					10	3	2	4	15	0
12	18	F	So.	2	4	3.0	1.8	1	2			51	22					14	7	0	4	8	0
13	21	M	So.	2	5	4.0	4.0			1		56	30	4				21	6	0	1	5	0
14	18	F	Fr.	2	7	5.0	4.6					50	22	1				11	3	0	5	3	2
15	25	M	Fr.	2	8	2.0	2.5					57	26					25	2	0	1	2	3
16	20	F	Jr.	2	9	3.7	4.0					52	25					18	2	0	7	2	2
17	20	M	Fr.	2	10	1.0	1.0	(E corrected)				47	23		X	X		24	4	0	3	1	0
18	21	M	So.	3	1	2.0	2.8					34	14		X	X		10	2	0	9	6	1
19	19	F	Fr.	3	3	3.0	3.0					50	9					24	3	0	3	3	1
20	18	F	So.	3	4	1.0	1.0		1			39	27	1				8	7	3	3	2	6
21	17	F	So.	3	5	1.0	1.7	1				45	16					11	10	1	2	4	3
22	18	F	Fr.	3	6	3.0	3.0		1			35	9					10	5	0	1	2	5
23	22	M	So.	3	7	3.0	2.8					51											
24	18	M	Fr.	3	8	3.0	3.4					52	27	1				16	4	0	9	3	1
25	40	F	So.	3	9	4.0	4.0					49	27					20	4	0	6	0	0
26	18	M	Jr.	3	10	4.7	4.8					47	28					18	5	0	2	4	0
27	19	F	Fr.	1	1	3.0	2.1	7	11			39	32	6	X	X	X	17	12	1	3	5	0
28	21	F	Fr.	1	2	2.0	2.8	1	2			46	26	3	X	X	X	12	11	2	0	1	0
29	20	M	Jr.	4	5	1.0	2.8					35	22					13	12	0	1	5	2
30	20	F	So.	1	3	4.0	3.6	2	7			37											
31	21	F	Jr.	1	5	4.0	3.0	2				60	20					10	4	0	7	7	3
32	19	M	Fr.	1	7	1.0	2.8					49	5					10	1	0	0	5	0
33	18	F	Fr.	1	9	2.0	2.0	1	1	1		43	20	1				7	6	1	6	0	1
34	18	F	Jr.	1	10	3.0	3.7					53	28	1				20	2	1	6	3	3
35	17	F	Fr.	2	1	4.0	3.1		1			47	26					8	6	2	1	1	3
36	23	M	Jr.	1	11	1.0	1.8	2	1	1	1	29	12					12	7	1	0	2	1
37	19	F	Fr.	2	2	1.0	2.0					36	18					6	8	2	2	2	1
38	18	F	Fr.	2	3	2.0	2.8					41	16					6	6	0	4	2	0
39	18	M	Fr.	2	6	1.7	1.7	(E corrected)				46	13					16	7	1	0	0	0
40	18	M	Fr.	2	7	1.0	1.0	(E corrected)				40	22	2			X	16	6	2	2	1	1

[*Publisher's Note:* To avoid folding, this table has been split. Normally there would be no break through the center.]

STATEMENT TEST					QUESTIONNAIRE RESULTS																						
O-2	O-0	O-	Own Score	True Score	Q1	Q2	Q3	Q4	Q5	Q6	Q7	Q8	Q9	Q10	Q11	Q12	Q13	Q14	Q15	Q16	Q17	Q18	Q19	Q20	Q21	Q22
					N	N	Y	N	N	N	N	Y	Y	N	Y	N	Y	N	YYY	N	ITF	a	N	ad	a	Y
		18	35	26	N	N	N	N	N	N	Y	Y	Y	N	Y	Y	N	N	NNN	Y	ITF	e	N	ad	a	N
		19	35	12	Y	N	Y	N	N	N	N	N	Y	N		N	Y	N	YYY				N		N	N
		4	51	42	N	N	N	N	N	N	Y	Y	Y	N	Y	N	Y	N	YNY	N	OTF	a	N	c-e	b	Y
		0	6	58	N	N	N	N	N	N	N	N	Y	N	N	N	Y	N	YYY	N	IAF	e	N	ce	f	N
					Y	N	N	N	N	N	N	N	Y	N	N	N	N	N	YNY	Y	OTF	e	a	ae	a	N
		8	39	32																						
		2	59	44	N	N	N	N	N	N	N	N	Y	N	N	N	Y	N	YYY				N	ac	a	N
					N	N	Y	N	N	N	Y	Y	N	Y	N	Y	N	N	YYY	Y	ITF	e	N	de	a	N
		15	42	26	Y	N	N	N	N	N	N	N	N	Y	N	N	N	N	YYY	N	ITF	e	N	ac	a	N
		6	49	28	Y	N	N	Y c	N	N	N	N	Y	Y	N	Y	Y	Y	YYY	N	ITF	e	N	ace	f	Y
		6	54	38	N	N	N	Y acd	N	N	N	N	N	Y	N	Y	N	Y	YYY	Y	IAS	e	N	ace	f	N
		6	60	46	N	N	N	N	N	N	Y	Y	N	N	N	N	N	Y	YYY	Y	OAF	e	N	f	a	
		16	38	32	N	N	N	N	N	N	N	N	N	Y	N	N	N	Y	YYY	Y	I F	e	N	N	f	N
		6	60	54	N	N	Y	N	N	N	Y	Y	Y	N	N	N	Y	N	YNY	Y	OAS	b	N	af	e	Y
		9	51	50	Y	N	N	N	N	N	N	Y	N	N	N	Y	Y	Y	YYY	Y	IAF	e	N	ab	a	N
		8	60	54	Y	N	Y	N	N	N	N	Y	Y	N	N	N	N	Y	YYY		OTF	e	N	a-c	g	N
		12	40	38	N	N	N	Y	N	N	N	N	b	Y	N	N	Y	N	NNN	N	IAF	d	a	c	a	Y
		6	61	54	Y	N	N	N	N	N	N	N	N	N	N	N	Y	Y			OTS	e	N	e	a	Y
		7	47	26	N	N	N	N	N	N	Y	N	Y	N	Y	N	Y	N	YNY	Y	AS	b	N	be	a	N
		9	53	26	N	N	N	N	N	N	N	Y	N	N	N	Y	N	Y	YNY	Y	A	e	N	b	a	N
		4	38	28	Y	N	Y	N	N	N	Y	Y	N	Y	N	Y	N	Y	YYY	O	OAA	e	N	a-f	a	Y
					Y	Y	Y	N	N	N	N	N	Y	N	Y	N	Y	Y	YYY	Y	AF	e	N	bc	e	Y
		4	53	56	Y	N	Y	N	N	N	Y	Y	N	Y	N	Y	N	Y	YYY	N	AF	a	N	ab	a	N
		10	54	52	N	N	Y	N a-e	Y	N	N	Y	N	N	N	Y	N	Y	YYY	N	AA	e	N	ad		N
		10	52	42	Y	N	N	Y	N	N	Y	Y	N	Y	N	Y	N	Y	YYY		A	e	N	Y	c	N
		1	68	40	Y	Y	N	N	N	N		Y	N	Y	N	Y	N	Y	YYY	Y	OTF	d	a	acf	a	N
		12	51	24	Y	Y	N	N	N	N	Y	N	Y	N	Y	N	Y	N	YYY	N		e	a	af	a	Y
		4	58	30	N	N	N	N	N	N	Y	Y	N	N	N	Y	N	N	NNN	N		a	a	a	b	Y
		9	45	34	N	N	Y	N	N	N	N	N	N	Y	N	Y	N	Y	YYY	Y	IAS	e	N	b	a	Y
		24	27	20	N	N	Y	N	N	N	Y	Y	N	N	N	N	N	N	NNN	N	IAS	e	N	abe	e	N
		19	36	26	Y	Y	N	N ab	N	Y	Y	Y	N	Y	N	N	N	N	NNY	Y	IAS	a	N	d-f	a	Y
		5	58	52	N	N	N	N ac	N	Y	Y	N	Y	N	N	N	N	N	NNY	Y	IAS	a	N	a-f	a	Y
		13	37	20	N	N	N	N	N	N	Y	N	Y	N	Y	N	N	N	NNN	N	IAS	e	N	b	c	N
		10	43	24	Y	Y	N	N	Y	N	Y	N	Y	N	Y	N	N	Y	NNY	Y	ITA	a	N	ac	a	Y
		19	37	16	N	N	N	Y	Y	N	Y	Y	N	Y	N	Y	N	Y	YYY	N	ITS	e	N	ae	e	N
		22	30	20	Y	N	Y	N	N	N	Y	Y	N	Y	N	N	N	N	NNN	N		N	b			N
		13	48	34	Y	Y	Y	N	N	N	Y	N	Y	N	Y	Y	Y	Y	YYY	Y	ITS	e	N	de	e	Y
		9	52	40	Y	N	N	Y	N	N	N	N	Y	N	Y	N	Y	N	YYY	N	OTA	e	N	ae	a	Y

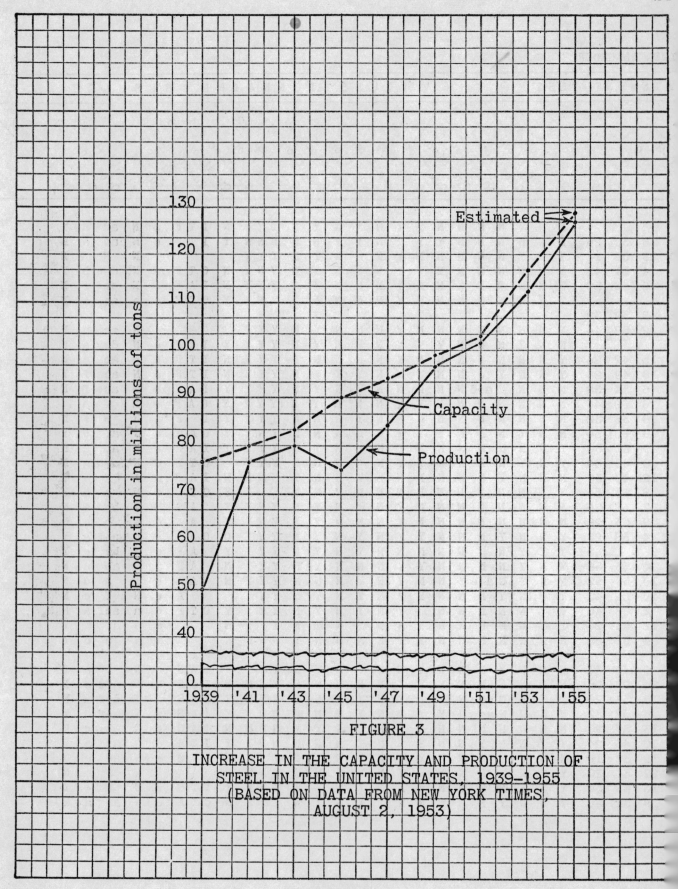

FIGURE 3

INCREASE IN THE CAPACITY AND PRODUCTION OF
STEEL IN THE UNITED STATES, 1939-1955
(BASED ON DATA FROM NEW YORK TIMES,
AUGUST 2, 1953)

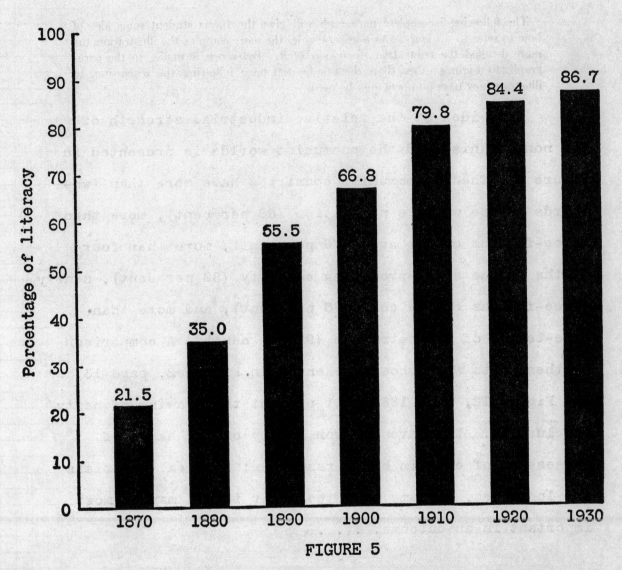

FIGURE 5

PERCENTAGE OF LITERACY AMONG NEW MEXICO POPULATION
TEN YEARS OF AGE AND OVER, 1870–1930 (FROM
SEYFRIED, PRINCIPLES OF RESEARCH)

The following incomplete paragraph will give the thesis student some idea of how to refer to a Figure. As a general rule, the more complex the illustration, the more detailed the contextual discussion of it. Reference is made, in the paragraph, to Figures other than the one on the page following the discussion, to illustrate how page numbers may be used.

Some idea of the relative industrial strength of the noncommunist and the communist worlds is presented in Figure 6. The noncommunist countries have more than two-thirds of the world's population (68 per cent), more than three-fourths of its area (76 per cent), more than four-fifths of the steel-producing capacity (82 per cent), nearly three-fourths of the coal (73 per cent), and more than nine-tenths of the petroleum (92 per cent). A comparison of these data with those presented in Figure 2, page 13, and Figure 12, page 126, will prevent the drawing of hasty conclusions. Wars are not won solely on the basis of possession of certain basic resources: critical materials and logistics, to name only two other items, may be most important in an outcome. . . .

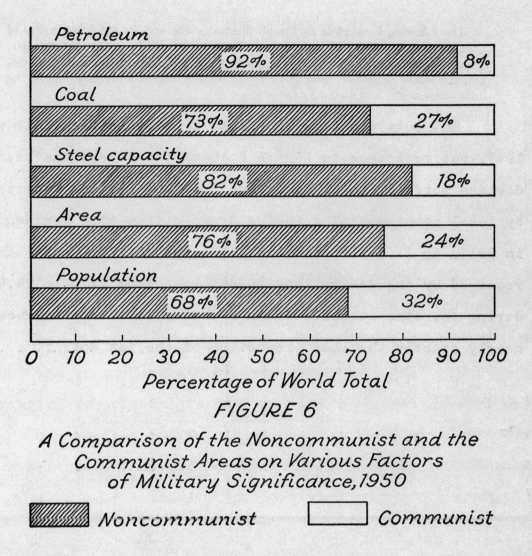

FIGURE 6

*A Comparison of the Noncommunist and the
Communist Areas on Various Factors
of Military Significance, 1950*

The following incomplete paragraph illustrates one way in which the writer of the thesis may refer to the contents of Figure 8. It will be noted that this particular Figure is rather simple, the major facts are self-evident; the contextual discussion would, therefore, tend to be brief. In the case of a complex Figure, the discussion might well run to a page or more.

Not only did taxes increase greatly between 1912 and 1947, but reference to Figure 8 shows that there has been a decided shift in their distribution. The portion received by local governmental agencies dropped from 57.9 per cent, in 1912, to 11.7 per cent, in 1947, whereas the percentage received by the federal government rose from 27.6 to 74.9 during the same period. State agencies continued to receive nearly exactly the same proportion of the tax dollar. . . .

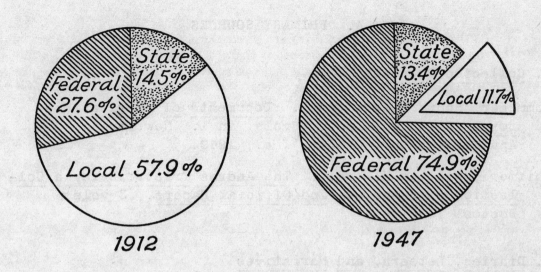

1912   1947

FIGURE 8

DISTRIBUTION OF THE AMERICAN TAX DOLLAR AMONG LOCAL,
STATE, AND FEDERAL GOVERNMENTS, 1912 and 1947
(FROM UNITED STATES DEPARTMENT OF
COMMERCE STATISTICS, 1947)

or

Figure 8. Distribution of the American tax dollar
among local, state, and federal governments, 1912 and 1947.
(From United States Department of Commerce Statistics, 1947.)

or

Figure 8. Distribution of the American tax dollar among
local, state, and federal governments, 1912 and 1947.
(From United States Department of Commerce Statistics,
1947.)

[Sample opening page of a bibliography.]

BIBLIOGRAPHY

A. PRIMARY SOURCES

1. Collected Documents

Commager, Henry Steele (ed.). Documents of American History. Fifth edition. 2 vols. in 1. New York: Appleton-Century-Crofts, Inc., 1949.

Whitmore, William H. (ed.). The Andros Tracts: Being a Collection of Pamphlets and Official Papers. 3 vols. Boston: 1868-74.

2. Diaries, Letters, and Narratives

Andrews, Charles McL. (ed.). Narratives of the Insurrections, 1675-1690. Original Narratives of Early American History. New York: Charles Scribner's Sons, 1915.

Bradford, William. Of Plymouth Plantation, 1620-1647. Edited by Samuel E. Morison. New York: Alfred A. Knopf, 1952.

Dreuillettes, Father Gabriel. "Narrative of a Journey to New England, 1650." Vol. XXXVI, pp. 83-111, in The Jesuit Relations and Allied Documents. . . 1610-1791. Edited by Reuben G. Thwaites. 73 vols. Cleveland: 1896-1901.

Dudley, Thomas. "Letter to the Countess of Lincoln," in Collections of the New Hampshire Historical Society, IV (1834), 224-49.

Homes, William. "Diary of Rev. William Homes of Chilmark, Martha's Vineyard, 1689-1746," New England Historical and Genealogical Register, XLVIII (1894), 446-53; XLIX (1895), 413-16; L (1896), 155-66.

Melville, Herman. Manuscript letters for the year 1849, in Folder No. 3 of seven folders of Melville manuscripts and letters in the Harvard College Library.

Allport, Gordon W. Personality: A Psychological Interpretation. New York: Henry Holt and Company, 1937. 588 pp.
  A general treatise on the nature of personality by an
authoritative writer in the field.

_____, and Leo J. Postman. The Psychology of Rumor. New
York: Henry Holt and Company, 1947. 247 pp.
  An analysis of the nature of rumor, the psychological
mechanisms of its dissemination, and the means of con-
trolling its spread.

American Association of School Administrators. Morale for a
Free World. Twenty-second Year Book. Washington, D.C.:
American Association of School Administrators, 1938.
461 pp.
  A consideration of the problems of developing proper
attitudes for democratic government among school chil-
dren; prepared by the Commission on Education for
Morale.

Anshen, Ruth Nanda (ed.). The Family: Its Function and
Destiny. Science of Culture Series, Vol. 5. New York:
Harper and Brothers, 1949. 443 pp.
  A valuable contribution to the study of the family,
in the form of a symposium of articles by Ruth Benedict,
E. F. Frazier, Erich Fromm, Ralph Linton, and others.

Archer, Gleason Leonard. Big Business and Radio. New York:
American Historical Company, 1939. 503 pp.
  A historical survey-analysis of corporate control of
American radio.

Bartlett, Frederic Charles. Political Propaganda. Cambridge, Eng.: Cambridge University Press, 1940. 158 pp.
  A careful analysis of the nature, dissemination,
and effects of political propaganda.

_____, et al. (eds.). The Study of Society: Methods and
Problems. New York: The Macmillan Company, 1939.
498 pp.
  A symposium by seventeen British psychologists, an-
thropologists, and sociologists, offering concrete
guidance to investigators in these fields.

Benedict, Ruth. Patterns of Culture. Boston: Houghton
Mifflin Company, 1934. 291 pp.
  A brilliant study of the nature of culture and its
impact on the institutions and functioning of societies.

FOOTNOTES

A. BOOKS

One author

[1]John C. Almack, Research and Thesis Writing (Boston: Houghton Mifflin Company, 1930), p. 218.

Two or three authors

[2]Witt Bowden, Michael Karpovich, and Abbott Payson Usher, An Economic History of Europe Since 1750 (New York: American Book Company, 1937), p. 422.

More than three authors

[3]Charles H. Johnston and others [or, et al.], The Modern High School (New York: Charles Scribner's Sons, 1914), pp. 603-14.

No author

[4]The School of Good Manners (New London, Connecticut: 1715), p. 7.

Edition

[5]Norman L. Munn, Psychology: The Fundamentals of Human Adjustment (second edition; Boston: Houghton Mifflin Company, 1951), pp. 365-69.

Editor, compiler, translator

[6]C. O. Sylvester Mawson (ed.), Roget's International Thesaurus of English Words and Phrases (New York: Thomas Y. Crowell Company, 1925), p. 314.

[7]Ina Ten Eyck Firkins (comp.), Index to Short Stories (second edition; New York: H. W. Wilson Company, 1923), pp. 422-67.

[8]William Bradford, Of Plymouth Plantation, 1620-1647, ed. Samuel E. Morison (New York: Alfred A. Knopf, 1952), p. 18.

[9]W. H. D. Rouse (trans.), Homer: The Iliad (New York: The New American Library, 1950), p. 61.

[10]Adolf Hitler, Mein Kampf, trans. Ralph Manheim (Boston: Houghton Mifflin Company, 1943), pp. 389-90.

Several volumes

[11]Paul Monroe (ed.), A Cyclopedia of Education (New York: The Macmillan Company, 1911), I, 345; II, 16-35.

BIBLIOGRAPHICAL ENTRIES

A. BOOKS

→ Almack, John C. Research and Thesis Writing. Boston:
Houghton Mifflin Company, 1930. 310 pp. [Or, Pp. vii+
310; or omit number of pages.]

→ Bowden, Witt, Michael Karpovich, and Abbott Payson Usher.
An Economic History of Europe Since 1750. New York:
American Book Company, 1937.

→ Johnston, Charles H., and others [or, et al.]. The Modern
High School. New York: Charles Scribner's Sons, 1914.

→ The School of Good Manners. New London, Connecticut: 1715.

→ Munn, Norman L. Psychology: The Fundamentals of Human
Adjustment. Second edition. Boston: Houghton Mifflin
Company, 1951.

→ Mawson, C. O. Sylvester (ed.). Roget's International
Thesaurus of English Words and Phrases. New York:
Thomas Y. Crowell Company, 1925.

→ Firkins, Ina Ten Eyck (comp.). Index to Short Stories.
Second edition. New York: H. W. Wilson Company, 1923.

→ Bradford, William. Of Plymouth Plantation, 1620-1647.
Edited by Samuel E. Morison. New York: Alfred A. Knopf,
1952.

→ Rouse, W. H. D. (trans.). Homer: The Iliad. New York: The
New American Library (Mentor Books), 1950.

→ Hitler, Adolf. Mein Kampf. Trans. Ralph Manheim. Boston:
Houghton Mifflin Company, 1943.

→ Monroe, Paul (ed.). A Cyclopedia of Education. 5 vols.
New York: The Macmillan Company, 1911.

FOOTNOTES

Several volumes,
separate titles

[12]Vernon Louis Parrington, The Romantic Revolution in America, 1800-1860 (Vol. II of Main Currents of American Thought. 3 vols.; New York: Harcourt, Brace and Company, 1927-30), p. 89.

Secondary source
citation

[13]Archer B. Hulbert, Portage Paths (Cleveland: Arthur H. Clark, 1903), p. 181, citing Jesuit Relations and Allied Documents, Vol. LIX, p. 41.

B. BOOKS: PARTS OF SERIES

Volume an organic
part of series

[14]Max Farrand, The Fathers of the Constitution (Vol. XIII of The Chronicles of America Series, ed. Allen Johnson. 50 vols.; New Haven: Yale University Press, 1918-21), p. 163.

Volume in loose
relation to series

[15]Ira B. Cross, Stuart Daggett, and Carl C. Plehn, The Dependent Aged in San Francisco (University of California Publications in Economics, Vol. V, No. 1. Berkeley, California: University of California Press, 1928), p. 110.

[16]C. H. Judd, Problems of Education in the United States (Recent Social Trends Monographs. New York: McGraw-Hill Book Company, Inc., 1933), pp. 13-55.

[17]Walter Havighurst, Upper Mississippi: A Wilderness Saga (in The Rivers of America Series, ed. Constance Lindsay Skinner. New York: Farrar and Rinehart, 1937), p. 111.

C. PUBLICATIONS OF THE GOVERNMENT, LEARNED SOCIETIES, AND OTHER ORGANIZATIONS

Organization the
author

[18]National Industrial Conference Board, Vacation and Holiday Practices (Studies in Personnel Policy No. 75. New York: National Industrial Conference Board, 1946), p. 5.

No author given
(or alternate form
of above)

[19]Vacation and Holiday Practices (Studies in Personnel Policy No. 75. New York: National Industrial Conference Board, 1946), p. 5.

BIBLIOGRAPHICAL ENTRIES

→ Parrington, Vernon Louis. The Romantic Revolution in
    America, 1800-1860. Vol. II of Main Currents in
    American Thought. 3 vols. New York: Harcourt, Brace
    and Company, 1927-30.

→ Hulbert, Archer B. Portage Paths. Cleveland: Arthur H.
    Clark, 1903.

B. BOOKS: PARTS OF SERIES

→ Farrand, Max. The Fathers of the Constitution. Vol. XIII
    of The Chronicles of America Series. Edited by Allen
    Johnson. 50 vols. New Haven: Yale University Press,
    1918-21.

→ Johnson, Allen (ed.). The Chronicles of America Series.
    50 vols. New Haven: Yale University Press, 1918-21.

→ Cross, Ira H., Stuart Daggett, and Carl C. Plehn. The
    Dependent Aged in San Francisco. University of
    California Publications in Economics, Vol. V, No. 1.
    Berkeley, California: University of California Press,
    1928.

→ Judd, C. H. Problems of Education in the United States.
    Recent Social Trends Monographs. New York: McGraw-Hill
    Book Company, Inc., 1933.

→ Havighurst, Walter. Upper Mississippi: A Wilderness Saga.
    In The Rivers of America Series, ed. Constance Lindsay
    Skinner. New York: Farrar and Rinehart, 1937.

C. PUBLICATIONS OF THE GOVERNMENT, LEARNED SOCIETIES,
AND OTHER ORGANIZATIONS

→ National Industrial Conference Board. Vacation and Holiday
    Practices. Studies in Personnel Policy No. 75. New
    York: National Industrial Conference Board, 1946.

→ Vacation and Holiday Practices. Studies in Personnel Policy
    No. 75. New York: National Industrial Conference Board,
    1946.

FOOTNOTES

Part of a report

[20]G. M. Wilson, "A Survey of the Social and Business Use of Arithmetic," Second Report of the Committee on Minimal Essentials in Elementary School Subjects, Sixteenth Yearbook of the National Society for the Study of Education, Part I (Bloomington, Illinois: Public School Publishing Company, 1917), pp. 20-22.

Govt. publication, individual author

[21]Vincent B. Phelan, Care and Repair of the House, National Bureau of Standards, United States Department of Commerce, Circular 489 (Washington: Government Printing Office, 1950), pp. 41-79.

Govt. publication, bureau the author

[22]United States Bureau of the Census, Seventeenth Census of the United States: 1950. Population, Vol. II (Washington: Government Printing Office, 1952), p. 33.

Congressional hearings

[23]United States Congress, Senate, Committee on the Judiciary, Federal Construction Contract Act, Hearings before Subcommittee, 82d Congress, 2d Session, on S. 2907, April 29-June 3, 1952 (Washington: Government Printing Office, 1952), p. 286. [Abbreviations U.S., Cong., and Sess. are often permissible.]

D. PERIODICALS

Standard form

[24]William Hard, "The Fight at Niagara," The Reader's Digest, LXIII (August, 1953), 30.

Variant form

[25]Nancy E. Scott, "The Effects of the Higher Education of Women Upon the Home," American Journal of Sociology, 32:257, September, 1926.

Volume not given; continued article

[26]Eugene Kinkead, "Egg Is All," The New Yorker, June 20, 1953, pp. 32-55; June 27, 1953, pp. 32-54.

E. ESSAYS AND ARTICLES IN COLLECTIONS

Essay in collection by one author

[27]Bertrand Russell, "Western Civilization," In Praise of Idleness and Other Essays (New York: W. W. Norton and Company, Inc., 1935), p. 182.

Essay in collection; no editor given

[28]H. R. Wagner, "Hispanic Americana in the John Carter Brown Library," Essays Honoring Lawrence C. Wroth (Portland, Me.: Anthoensen Press, 1951), pp. 91-96.

BIBLIOGRAPHICAL ENTRIES

→ Wilson, G. M. "A Survey of the Social and Business Use of Arithmetic," Second Report of the Committee on Minimal Essentials in Elementary School Subjects, pp. 20-22. Sixteenth Yearbook of the National Society for the Study of Education, Part I. Bloomington, Illinois: Public School Publishing Company, 1917.

→ Phelan, Vincent B. Care and Repair of the House. National Bureau of Standards, United States Department of Commerce, Circular 489. Washington: Government Printing Office, 1950.

→ United States Bureau of the Census. Seventeenth Census of the United States: 1950. Population, Vol. II. Washington: Government Printing Office, 1952.

→ United States Congress, Senate, Committee on the Judiciary. Federal Construction Contract Act. Hearings before Subcommittee, 82d Congress, 2d Session, on S. 2907, April 29-June 3, 1952. Washington: Government Printing Office, 1952. [Abbreviations U.S., Cong., and Sess. are often permissible.]

D. PERIODICALS

→ Hard, William. "The Fight at Niagara," The Reader's Digest, LXIII (August, 1953), 27-32.

→ Scott, Nancy E. "The Effects of the Higher Education of Women Upon the Home," American Journal of Sociology, 32:256-63, September, 1926.

→ Kinkead, Eugene. "Egg Is All," The New Yorker, June 20, 1953, pp. 32-55; June 27, 1953, pp. 32-54.

E. ESSAYS AND ARTICLES IN COLLECTIONS

→ Russell, Bertrand. "Western Civilization," In Praise of Idleness and Other Essays. New York: W. W. Norton and Company, Inc., 1935. Pp. 181-203.

→ Wagner, H. R. "Hispanic Americana in the John Carter Brown Library," Essays Honoring Lawrence C. Wroth. Portland, Me.: Anthoensen Press, 1951. Pp. 72-108.

FOOTNOTES

Essay in collection; editor and series given

[29]Jean Seznec, "Paul Claudel and the Sarcophagus of the Muses," _Perspectives of Criticism_, Harry Levin, editor (Harvard Studies in Comparative Literature, No. 20.   Cambridge: Harvard University Press, 1950), pp. 10-11.

F.   ENCYCLOPEDIA ARTICLES

Signed article

[30]Edward Sapir, "Language," _Encyclopaedia of the Social Sciences_ (New York: The Macmillan Company, 1933), IX, 159-62.

Signed with identifiable initials

[31]William Spry, "Homestead and Exemption Laws," _Encyclopaedia Britannica_ (14th ed.), XI, 705.

Unsigned

[32]"Vaccination," _Encyclopaedia Britannica_ (14th ed.), XXII, 921-23.

G.   UNPUBLISHED MATERIALS

Mimeographed

[33]Julian C. Aldrich, "How to Construct and Use a Resource Unit" (New York: Joint Council on Economic Education, 1951), p. 7.   (Mimeographed.)

Paper read but unpublished

[34]Harold C. Holland, "Dynamics: Some New Perspectives" (paper read at the National Science Laboratory, Northtown, New Jersey, May 11, 1953).

Dissertation

[35]Frank L. James, "An Analysis of the Application of Certain Relief Measures in Los Angeles" (unpublished Master's thesis, The University of Southern California, Los Angeles, 1952), p. 112.

H.   NEWSPAPERS

General citations

[36]Editorial in the _Los Angeles Times_, February 27, 1946.

[37]News item in the _Los Angeles Times_, April 30, 1950.

Interpolation

[38]Associated Press dispatch, _Witfield_ [New Mexico] _Daily_, November 6, 1912.

Signed article in special section

[39]John Lehmann, "T. S. Eliot Talks About Himself and the Drive to Create," _The New York Times Book Review_, November 29, 1953, pp. 5, 44.

BIBLIOGRAPHICAL ENTRIES

→ Seznec, Jean. "Paul Claudel and the Sarcophagus of the
    Muses," Perspectives of Criticism, Harry Levin, editor.
    Harvard Studies in Comparative Literature, No. 20.
    Cambridge: Harvard University Press, 1950. Pp. 1-17.

F. ENCYCLOPEDIA ARTICLES

→ Sapir, Edward. "Language," Encyclopaedia of the Social
    Sciences, IX, 155-69. New York: The Macmillan Company,
    1933.

→ Spry, William. "Homestead and Exemption Laws," Encyclo-
    paedia Britannica (14th ed.), XI, 704-5.

→ "Vaccination," Encyclopaedia Britannica (14th ed.), XXII,
    921-23.

G. UNPUBLISHED MATERIALS

→ Aldrich, Julian C. "How to Construct and Use a Resource
    Unit." New York: Joint Council on Economic Education,
    1951. (Mimeographed.)

→ Holland, Harold C. "Dynamics: Some New Perspectives."
    Paper read at the National Science Laboratory,
    Northtown, New Jersey, May 11, 1953.

→ James, Frank L. "An Analysis of the Application of Certain
    Relief Measures in Los Angeles." Unpublished Master's
    thesis, The University of Southern California, Los
    Angeles, 1952.

H. NEWSPAPERS

File Los Angeles Times, January, 1946-December, 1952.

Single issue Los Angeles Times, April 30, 1950.

→ Witfield [New Mexico] Daily, November 6, 1912.

→ Lehmann, John. "T. S. Eliot Talks About Himself and the
    Drive to Create," The New York Times Book Review,
    November 29, 1953, pp. 5, 44.

INDEX

112

8997